WE WERE HERE FIRST, KID!

WE WERE HERE FIRST, KID!

A PRACTICAL GUIDE TO HAPPY PARENTING

By Christie Mellor

**SIMON &
SCHUSTER**

London · New York · Sydney · Toronto · Dublin

A VIACOM COMPANY

I would like to gratefully acknowledge my friend Sarah Wingfield, whose noisy enthusiasm for the first thirteen pages of this book encouraged me to write the rest. The good and wise Jack Jensen, who said, 'Send it our way', and Jay Schaefer, a marvellous editor and fine cocktail companion. Linda Sunshine for her generous advice; the talented and unstinting Jim Dean, for all his help; Clara Rodriguez, for bringing me more paper dolls and reading all those e-mails; Maria Bustillos and Susanna Thompson for the infectious optimism; Toni DeVito for never forgetting the sprig of mint; and The Stump™ (but the older, funnier one). A thousand thanks to my very own Richard Goldman, for the kicky title, as well as for his unflagging support, keen eye, musical interludes, and doing of the dishes. To Edison and Atticus, the best boys ever. And a very heartfelt thank-you to the many parents and children without whom this book would have been unnecessary.

First published by Simon & Schuster UK Ltd, 2005
A Viacom Company

3 5 7 9 10 8 6 4 2

Simon & Schuster UK Ltd
Africa House
64–78 Kingsway
London WC2B 6AH

www.simonsays.co.uk

Simon & Schuster Australia, Sydney

A CIP catalogue record for this book is available from the British Library

ISBN 0-7432-6330-8

Printed and bound in Great Britain by Mackays of Chatham plc

This Book is dedicated
with much love
to Mike and Mary-Gin Mellor,
the original
Three-Martini Parents.

• CONTENTS •

· HELPFUL HINTS! ·

· RECIPES ·

IN PRAISE OF GROWN-UP TIME

IT HAS COME TO MY ATTENTION THAT CHILDREN HAVE become the centre of our universe.

Gone are the days when a small person of tender age would do as he or she was asked, good-naturedly and obediently, and the rest of the time would sit quietly reading or practising a simple cross-stitch. The child was able to carry on a lively and friendly conversation with a grown-up, when asked; but with equal good nature the youngster would disport himself to a quiet corner when it appeared that the grown-ups were converging. He might be trotted out to say his hellos, perhaps to recite, possibly to help serve drinks or pass cocktail peanuts. He might sit on a lap, but only if requested by a familiar grown-up. He never presumed.

One wasn't required to transport the little children hither and thither, here to football practice, there to a 'playdate' (may the chipper mummy who coined that particular term forever rot in a hell of eternally colicky babies).

One wasn't required to endure swarms of youngsters teeming over the hors d'oeuvres, begging for refreshment just as one was about to take that first heady sip of one's ice-cold martini. There was water, and they knew how to retrieve it.

Let us be perfectly frank. You were here first. You are sharing your house with them, your food, your time, your books. Somewhere, in fairly recent memory, we have lost sight of that fact. Somehow a pint-sized velvet revolution was waged right under our very noses, and the grown-ups quietly handed over the reins. We have made concession after concession, until it appears that well-educated, otherwise intelligent adults have abdicated their rightful place in the world, and the littlest inmates have taken over the asylum. Remember when we couldn't wait to grow up so *we* could be in charge?

It is time to set this madly spinning orb back on its axis. This book is for parents; for parents-to-be who have assumed that the world as they know it must necessarily change with the imminent introduction of a small child into their life; and for the newlywed couple who contemplate conception but fear that sharing hearth and home with a young tot will only lead to sleeplessness, high-pitched fits of screaming, and the dearth of adult companionship for the remainder of their days. This book is meant for all the grown-ups who have, against all reason, decided to welcome a tiny bundle of joy into their home, but who rightly feel that a complete lifestyle makeover is too high a price to pay.

It is also a chance for me, as a parent, to get an awful lot off my chest regarding what I consider to be a great many silly parents out there, doing a great many very silly things.

Simply put, you deserve a little time of your own, a little grown-up time, time to do whatever it is you like to do by yourself, or with friends. I don't mean stealing a guilty moment to scan the headlines while you gulp down half a cup of scalding coffee, accompanied by the persistent whine of a petulant four-year-old. It is not that you would be stealing this time from your precious child. It is not your child's time you are stealing; it is your time, and you get to have some of it for yourself.

There is no guilt in craving social situations that aren't wholly centred around everyone's children. There is no shame in explaining to your children that they should go and find Something to Do, that the grown-ups are having grown-up talk, that they, the little children, need to go somewhere and be little children. Whether you would like to share a portion of your time with one grown-up or a party of them, or simply enjoy a moment alone, it is time to exert a little autonomy and encourage some in your child. This book explains how. It's time to warm up the ice cubes, curl up on the sofa, and send darling Caspar into the other room to play by himself. Mummy and Daddy need a little break.

ETIQUETTE FOR FIRST-TIME PARENTS

SOME PARENTS BELIEVE THAT THEIR OFFSPRING ARE channeling the very angels, and who can blame them, as little Clementine and young Archie are such dolls? Please, I encourage you to keep this information to yourself. Your darling Finlay may wear a golden halo, and I know the temptation is great to point it out to friends and strangers alike, but you must not. Just as it would be bad form to discuss one's personal saviour at a dinner party full of atheists, it would be wise to assume that even many fellow parents will stare with frozen smiles when the serene first-timer says in that smug, knowing way, 'Having Hayley has just changed my life. Wow. I am learning so much from her'. If by this you mean you are learning to stay up all night crying, to squirt poo out through your trouser leg, and to vomit at random on people's shoulders, then you will certainly have a sympathetic audience. If, however, you would like us to infer that you have embarked upon some kind of Spiritual Journey after giving birth, then I would urge you to explore your journey silently, or with other like-minded adults. Also, refrain from announcing in a room full of new parents, 'Oh, little Daisy has been sleeping through the night since she was three weeks old!' Do not share this joyful news, for your own safety.

- **CHAPTER 1** -

SAYING NO TO YOUR CHILD:
IT'S A KICK!

ONCE MY SON WAS PLAYING WITH ANOTHER BOY, WHOM I
will call 'Butchie'. Butchie thought it would be a good idea to
punch my son repeatedly in the arm until my son cried.
Butchie's father, who witnessed the event, pulled his son aside
and told him that it was 'inappropriate' for Butchie to hit
his friend repeatedly in the arm. He said it very calmly and
reasonably. It was just not appropriate to beat up his friend.

I wanted to put in my two pennies' worth and say that I
thought it was inappropriate to mince words when speaking
to a four-year-old. Butchie had hurt his friend and that was a
bad thing to do, and he should say he's sorry. Being exces-
sively polite, I didn't say anything, but I ask you, why is it so
difficult for an intelligent grown-up man to tell his son that
his son did something wrong?

If you're four years old, pulling your trousers down at the
dinner table is 'inappropriate'; making farting noises at a tea
party is 'inappropriate'. If you're six years old, making farting
noises at a tea party is very rude. If I might be so judgmental,

16

punching your friend in the arm is mean. It's bad. You hurt your friend, and you shouldn't hurt people. What is so awful about letting your children know this? Should we keep it a big secret and hope they find out one day by accident? Running your friend down with a toy tractor and trying to choke him is also a bad thing to do, if I may be so bold, which is what happened to my son with another child. (My son mixed with some rough trade at the age of four.) In that particular instance, the child ran to his mother, who picked him up and, hugging him tightly, said in a sweet, singsongy voice, 'Oh, darling, you shouldn't do that, that's not nice. Okay? Aww.' I'm not kidding. Her son was choking my child, and she cuddled him and told him that everything was all right. She was so worried his feelings might be bruised, because I seemed so darn angry about the tyre treads on my son's forehead. Her little sociopath just looked at me and smiled from the safe haven of his mother's arms.

This mother subscribed to a certain theory of childrearing whereby a child should never have to say he's sorry, as that would somehow foster low self-esteem. In addition, this theory holds that one should never say NO to a child. Perhaps it would be demeaning, or stunt his creative spirit. There are many parents who subscribe to this theory. There are also many who follow the spirit, if not the letter, of this brand of childrearing, parents who simply do not say no to their children, because, well, they get such a negative reaction. Kids really, really don't like it when you say no to them. Some of them make a big fuss, in hopes that the parent will have a change of heart. If the no easily turns into 'Well, all right,' the child will have learned that with some well-timed protest the tide against him can turn.

To what depths have we sunk as parents? We have become ineffectual lap dogs to our children, with all the power and authority of retired security guards. We are bigger than they are. We are supposed to be running things. If you don't start saying no to your children as if you mean it, and you don't start now, the tantrums will only get worse. Children really do want to be told no, despite their protestations. If they are never told no, they will keep doing louder and more unpleasant things until somebody does tell them no, and when that somebody finally does tell them no, in addition to telling them that they are behaving like horrid brats, they will have finally found a grown-up that they can respect. With any luck, that somebody will be you, rather than some cherished family friend, whose visits will have become strangely few and far between. Learn to say no to your children while they are still young and somewhat malleable, and it will be like money in the bank when they reach those really unbearable hormone-laden years.

WHEN YOU ARE THE VICTIM
OF YOUR OWN CHILD

TIME AND AGAIN I HAVE SEEN THREE-, FOUR-, AND FIVE-YEAR-old children punching their mummies in the face, slapping them across the head, and kicking them in the shins, while the mummies say in calm, gentle voices, 'Darling – ow – please don't hit me. Sweetie, please. What's the matter, darling? Are you having angry feelings, sweetheart? Ow.' The mothers continue attempting to soothe the little savages into submission with hugs and kisses, while dodging tiny but vicious blows.

Would you accept this behavior from a friend? From your spouse? If the answer to those questions is a resounding 'Yes!' then your problems are beyond my limited scope, but if you, like most women, would perhaps bristle at your husband socking you in the jaw because you said that there were no more biscuits in the house, then think about what kind of message you are sending your child.

The first time your sweet munchkin hauls back and wallops you across the face, let him know in no uncertain terms that hitting people is not an acceptable manner of expressing himself. If it's not okay to hit his friends or his siblings, it certainly should not be okay to slap Mummy on the head.

Mothers, have a little self-respect! It will not only save you a few black eyes now, it will help you nurture a kind and thoughtful child who will take good care of his dear mama when she is old and grey.

Practise saying no! *firmly and consistently in front of a mirror, or with your spouse in the privacy of your bedroom. Develop a 'stern' look, much like the one your mother used to use on you when you had reached the limit. Remember that look? The look that could shut anyone up from twenty feet? The look that, if they were on the business end of it, would send neighbouring children scurrying home, suddenly remembering homework and chores they had forgotten to do? Perfect that look. Develop a series of 'looks'. Your 'look' will serve you well, and is so much fun to do!*

CHAPTER 2

THE CHILDPROOF HOUSE: HOW TO KNOW IF YOU'VE GONE TOO FAR

I ONCE ATTENDED A LOVELY DINNER PARTY AT THE HOUSE of a couple who had two small children. It was the cusp of the evening, the adults were enjoying dessert and coffee, and the children were happily tucked away in a far corner of the house viewing a videotape. I discreetly excused myself from the table and found my way to the powder room.

I immediately turned around and made my way straight back to my hostess's chair, where I delicately explained to her that I had been unable to raise the lid of the toilet seat.

Now, I am no rocket scientist, but I have had a modicum of education. I have mastered the cash machine, can use a computer, and am even able to navigate the Internet without too much difficulty. I can open jars, install window treatments, and build shelves that are reasonably level, despite what you may have heard. I'd say I have a pretty good handle on basic tools and hardware. Yet there I was, with a bladder full to bursting, unable to free the toilet lid from its complex restraint system, a system apparently designed to foil even the most cunning safecracker.

With a chuckle, I was shown that all I had to do was reach under this, unlatch that, and release the springcatch below the lip of the toilet bowl. Utterly abashed, I laughingly agreed that I was indeed an idiot, and my hostess vacated the loo before I peed on her floor.

Can it possibly be true that an untold number of toddlers are actually drowning in the toilets of the developed world? Might it not be a good idea to explain to one's two-year-old child that she mustn't put her head in the potty and leave it there? Has anyone thought that perhaps a simple hook on the door to the bathroom might be the answer to this silent epidemic?

An entire industry has sprung up based solely upon the fears of the new parent, that of 'childproofing' one's house. Lest new parents be squeamish about reprimanding their toddler for playing near the stove, just in case one can't bear the idea of having to yell at little Max to get the fork out of the electrical socket, we now have a host of experts who will enter our houses, hide the sharp edges, and smooth over the rough spots. They will install a Bubbles the Elephant Spout Cover, in case your child knocks his head into that naughty bathtap while you are bathing him. They will convince you that you are a bad mother if you do not order lots of unsightly foam padding with which to decorate your nice furniture. They honestly believe that you should remove the knobs on your cooker 'when not in use', unless of course you plan to purchase their convenient Stove Guard. They worry that you habitually run around the house with open pots of hot grease, an activity in which I have never knowingly participated; but if I did, I would certainly tell my children to step aside while I sprinted through with the sizzling bacon drippings.

A certain amount of childproofing is reasonable. One may find helpful hints for the new parent in every book on childrearing, usually with the suggestion that one crawl around on the floor in order to see the house from the child's point of view. This can be a delightful activity to undertake with one's spouse, as it often leads to horseplay and intimate rolling about while you search for electrical outlets and any frayed, bare wires. You will not only spot a few hidden dangers, you will invariably find lost earrings, that book you misplaced last summer, and enough loose change for a couple of nice espressos. It will also give you a chance to clean up the giant dustballs, untangle that mess of cords, and remove the obvious hazards (plastic dry-cleaning bag, shards of broken glass, olive pick) that might harm your child. I understand that we mustn't leave multi-coloured thumbtacks lying about, and if it says, 'Keep out of reach of children', then you'd best keep it out of reach, along with your mother's crystal sherry decanter and your prized drill bits. Affixing padding on the corner of every table, however, is taking it too far.

Perhaps you think that if you hide the pointy things they will go away, but you are making a dreadful mistake. There are sharp, pointy things out there, and not just in your house. I would suggest that you point out these pointy things to your youngsters, and explain that they should not run with, run into, or swallow these pointy things. They need to learn, and they will not learn if you are hiding things under rubber bumpers and behind doorknob guards. It is not necessary to have an intricate locking device on your napkin drawer, unless your child is prone to ramming wads of paper products down his throat.

All those expensive childproofing locks that you think are securing your arsenal of nail clippers, screwdrivers, and kebab skewers are nothing more than high-powered magnets for children, who have usually worked out how to unlock all of the more complicated ones by the age of two or three anyway. You might as well festoon all your drawers and cabinets with brightly coloured flags that say 'Hey, You! Fun and Danger in Here!'

Your child will scrape his knees on gravel, repeatedly. That is why we have colourful plastic bandages. He will soon come to know and fear the dancing blue flames on the hob. Your child may even run headlong into the edge of the dining room table, and the largest black-and-blue egg you have ever seen may sprout on his forehead, but he will only run into it once. And honestly, if he keeps running into it, it won't be because he hasn't been painfully warned. One should welcome the little accidents and near accidents that teach one's child about danger and instruct him, often dramatically, in how to avoid it. If an incident should befall your child, and should this injury require stitches, you can relax with the knowledge that having a childhood scar always makes a person much more interesting as an adult.

Children are surprisingly adept at learning, and are, even at a very young age, able to understand when you tell them not to go under the sink because there is poison there, and if they touch it they will turn purple and die. If they are too young or too wilful to understand the simplest of warnings, then by all means, hide your ammonia and caustics and airfix glue where they can't get at them, but get a grip when you find yourself about to put a lock on the cutlery drawer. If you don't teach them now, do not be surprised when, forty years from now, your adult son electrocutes himself with a spoon, or drowns in the toilet, or repeatedly sets his hair on fire when using the stove.

As far as those irritating toilet-seat locks and drawer guards go, you not only run the risk of embarrassing your guests, you take all the fun out of going to the powder room at a party, since it is a universal habit to sneak a peek into the drawers and cabinets of every hostess's bathroom. Your guests will surmise that (a) You are afraid of having your hand lotion stolen, or (b) You are the most neurotic human on the planet.

PRACTICAL CHILDPROOFING

IT MAY BE THAT YOUR LITTLE DARLING CAN'T HELP POKING around all those drawers he has been admonished to avoid, and in doing so, he may come across a sharp set of fondue forks, one of which he will grab and test on his little arm. It will make a tiny impression in his skin that may surprise him, and through his tears, he will probably ask you what in the heck one does with such a tiny, sharp fork. You will tell him all about the wonders of crusty French bread dipped in melted cheese, and you will ask him to please put the fork away, as it is not a toy and it could hurt him. He will be happy to comply.

Repeat the above exercise with fish forks, kebab skewers, and silver cocktail picks, then send your well-informed youngster to the Tupperware cupboard, where he can make a nice, safe mess.

CHAPTER 3

BEDTIME:
IS FIVE-THIRTY TOO EARLY?

LETTING CHILDREN CHOOSE THEIR OWN BEDTIMES IS, simply put, insane. Why would one do such a thing? Why would a parent rob himself of a load of free time, in addition to robbing his child of some much-needed sleep?

I realize that some parents get home from work late and feel guilty that they haven't seen enough of their child, but really, you will be spending the entire weekend with these people, you spent last weekend with them, and you will probably get to enjoy their company for many weekends to come. The children need to sleep, and you need to put your feet up.

Often parents think that letting their child fall asleep 'naturally' is more, well, 'natural', although I find nothing natural about a six-year-old building a fortress out of the sofa pillows at ten o'clock at night.

Some parents simply haven't worked out that they have potential hours at their disposal; peaceful, unfettered, child-free hours. They have overlooked that magic time between, say, eight p.m. and one a.m. when books may be read, newspapers caught up with, novels written, and, of course, parties held. Instead, they will crawl into their rooms and collapse from utter exhaustion every night, mere minutes after putting the little ones down. Both parents and their children will wake up snappish and moody from not having a regular bedtime.

There is much that the grown-up evening has to offer, and the best way to ensure that you will have a grown-up evening is to enforce a strict, consistent, and reasonably early bedtime.

Enforcement only becomes a little tricky during the 'daylight savings' period, the time of year in which you must convince your child that, although the sun is brightly shining, it is 'So late!' and he must be 'So tired!'. Trust me, it is and he is. Provide a solid bedtime ritual and he will fall into his pillow happily at the appointed hour. Autumn, winter, and very early spring are good times to establish this appointed hour, as darkness falls somewhere around five o'clock. There is a chill in the air. Jimjams are produced, and donned. You and the little ones might curl up in front of a roaring fire, toast a few marshmallows, and read a few favourite books. The warm, sleepy, and slightly disoriented children then brush their teeth and pile into bed with plenty of time for you to prepare for company expected to arrive by eight-thirty.

When planning on getting together with friends for an evening, especially single friends or childless couples, assume that after a certain hour guests would be less than delighted to have a sleep-deprived child trotted out for their admiration and entertainment. There are exceptions to this rule. Perhaps you have a friend who genuinely likes children, or your child in particular. Then, by all means, plan an evening whereby the guest may arrive earlier and enjoy the company of your child for a brief period before bedtime. Better yet, plan a day-time visit.

If a child should wake, very late, to find you and your friends out on the patio swilling cocktails and smoking tobacco, do not be alarmed, or deterred from having an adult evening. If this particular child requires more than the cursory 'Nighty night and back to bed, you monkey', consider lifting the sleepy trespasser in your arms, letting him say his hellos and good-nights to the assembled guests, then taking him in and placing him firmly back in bed. You might suggest that the police are watching him, and that he must go back to sleep like a good child in order to avoid a stiff sentence in jail. Don't forget a goodnight kiss!

This is also a wonderful opportunity to refresh your lip-stick and empty the ashtrays before you rejoin your guests.

- CHAPTER 4 -

THE CHILD AT A SOCIAL EVENT

I AM NOT ESPOUSING A RETURN TO THE ERA WHEN CHILdren were seen and not heard – a lofty goal, but one which is now simply impractical. In fact, one should have conversations with the children from time to time, so that they will learn how to speak with confidence and enthusiasm, should a grown-up wish to have a thoughtful exchange.

They should know at an early age that taking an interest in the person with whom they are engaged in conversation is a charming trait that will serve them well. If your child cannot muster any genuine interest, then teaching him how to feign interest will make him appear to be a cleverer and more fascinating conversational partner. We are not wrong to expect more than grunts and coyly evasive answers.

Children should have a passing familiarity with a few topics of conversation, such as books they like to read, and why. For the prereader, an analysis of Dinosaurs versus Dragons might be an apt subject of conversation, or the excitement of Things That Have Wheels. For those youngsters already in school, Wind and Solar Energy, Insects versus Arachnids, and

possibly, How the Global Capitalist System Ruthlessly Exploits Children and Other Gullible People are subjects they are never too young to be conversant with.

On the other hand, there is the overly precocious 'little adult' who is eternally encouraged to join in with the grown-ups, having been told too many times he is 'beautiful' or 'so funny!' or 'exceedingly bright'. These tiny party crashers find it necessary to dominate the grown-ups' attention with a desperate display of their banter. We know children are naturally self-centered creatures. Aren't we all? But show-offs are show-offs, whether they are five or thirty-five.

Children should be disabused of the notion that the following behaviours are in any way 'Cute':

1. Commentary upon the personal grooming habits, hairstyle, or lipstick choice of a grown-up, however unfortunate. 'Children are so very honest!' may be a truism, but is it necessary to hear those truths? One must never mistake rudeness for honesty.
2. Circling the table at an alarming pace and singing/screaming/howling in an insistent tone while the grown-ups attempt to eat a meal.
3. A display of sarcasm beyond their years. If your five-year-old knows anything at all about the personal

lives of popular media personalities, can sing the questionable lyrics to a teen hit, or has perfected a sneering quality that her parents find hilarious, I would suggest a nice camping trip for the entire family, and perhaps a moratorium on television viewing for, say, a year.

If you would like to include your children, albeit briefly, at the start of whatever festivities you have planned, you might consider teaching them to pass a plate of hors d'oeuvres or distribute cocktail napkins. Such occupations should prevent the little darlings from displaying their expertise with under-arm farting, or exhorting the assembled guests to watch them gargle. If they are six or seven and capable of pouring liquid into a container the size of a cocktail shaker, then set them to a practical task such as mixing simple gin and tonics or pouring a whisky, neat or on the rocks. This is not only an aid to you, the hostess, but a practical exercise in hand-eye coordination.

To that end, I include a handy recipe that will help the more talented youngsters feel a part of all the exciting grown-up activity while perfecting a skill that will prove highly useful as they grow older.

OUR LITTLE TOT'S FIRST
MARTINI RECIPE

ALL YOUNG CHILDREN SHOULD KNOW HOW TO MAKE this delightful yet deceptively simple cocktail for their parents and other thirsty grown-ups who drop by around five o'clock. Glasses should be chilled until they're icy cold, and when asking about garnish preference the child should sweetly inquire, 'Olive or Twist?' Grown-ups will think he is making a funny literary joke, and then they'll laugh, and maybe give him tuppence.

Chill two martini glasses. Fill a shaker to the brim with ice, and add:

4 lugs fine gin
Splash of dry vermouth

Gently shake, strain, and pour into well-chilled glasses. Serve with an olive or twist of lemon. (For a Gibson, garnish with a cocktail onion.) Teach your youngster to say 'Cheers' at an early age, and he will be on the road to a successful social life!

CHAPTER 5

SCREAMING: IS IT NECESSARY?

I HAVE A DEAR FRIEND WHOSE CHILD OF FIFTEEN MONTHS
screams. Screams with a fervour forgotten by those grown-ups
not undergoing electroshock therapy. Screams when breakfast
is not placed before him fast enough. Screams when, finished
with his breakfast, he wishes to be freed from his high-chair
restraints, so that he might roam about and possibly bang on
the piano. Screams when his tired mama attempts to wrest him
from the piano keys, screams in joy at breaking from her grasp,
screams as he runs out of the door headlong into sharp objects
and pits of mud. Screaming is often a fact of life for a fifteen-
month-old child, and it must be tolerated, to a point, for it is
primal and necessary.

In children of three, four, five, six, or seven years, it is
just something that they have been getting away with for far
too long. That is why you must tell them to stop screaming
at the earliest age possible, though at first they may take very
little notice of you. By the age of three, or four, or five, their
little lungs have grown, and they are capable of inflicting mind-
numbing irritation, not to mention serious damage to the

grown-up eardrum. When grown-ups are about to engage in conversation and, need I say, that first welcome sip of their evening beverage, a piercing shriek emanating from a nearby youngster is not a happy addition to the ambience.

I have heard numerous reactions from parents to their screaming children, one of which is this simple but misguided admonition: 'Sweetheart! That is not our Inside Voice, that is our Outside Voice! We only use that voice *outside*.'

It is irresponsible to encourage screaming, inside or out. If the screamers are sent outside to scream, it will merely be a temporary respite, and your brief peace will soon be shattered by the shouts of anxious neighbours, passersby, and the policemen who have come to investigate. Screaming is a bad idea, indoors or out, and will end a cocktail party one way or another if it's not nipped in the bud.

I once knew a mother who, when faced with a screaming daughter, shrugged it off with a smile, explaining, 'Girls scream'. Apparently boys growl and roar, and are made of puppy dog tails, while it is acceptable for little sugar-spun females to engage in high-pitched fits of screaming, because, after all, 'Girls scream. What can you do?'

Yelling, the only slightly less startling version of screaming, is just as much of an annoyance when one is in the middle of an interesting conversation with a grown-up. Unless little Timmy has fallen down the well or the house is on fire, there is no need to holler full bore while standing two feet away from a parent. Your child should be reminded of this in no uncertain terms before you decide it would be fun to entertain a group of adults who might value what is left of their hearing.

Sadly, the use of child-sized muzzles has never quite caught on, though I can't see why not. If your child is prone to yelling and/or screaming, especially in a room full of visiting grown-ups, gently set down your glass, take him firmly by the hand, and lead him to a quiet corner. Explain that vocalizing at such a high decibel level is not an entertainment option. If your child feels the need to scream out loud, then he must find a secluded cupboard, or a distant, uninhabited corner of the house, and there he may scream to his little heart's content. Explain that when he is older, he may go to the railway sidings, or to a motorway overpass, or a psychiatrist's office, and scream at the passing trains, vehicles, or psychiatrist; but until that glorious day has arrived, screaming must be a private pursuit. When your child realizes that he will be all alone in some dark, cramped cupboard, free of an adult audience, he will soon tire of the sport, and move on to quieter activities.

CHAPTER 6

YOUR CHILD'S LIFE:
NOW AVAILABLE ON DVD!

CERTAINLY YOU ARE ALLOWED TO MAKE A RECORDED HIS-
tory of your life. Certainly you are free to videotape your
spouse brushing her teeth on your Mexican holiday, or digi-
tally record your child eating dirt and singing off-key, but
please, don't expect me to sit down and watch it for two hours
at a party. I already know far too many people who cannot
seem to get through one Sports Day, one Nativity Play, one
Christmas morning, one holiday, birthday party, or school
assembly, without some sort of recording device strapped to
their arm. Whatever happened to taking a few fuzzy snapshots?

I attended my child's costume 'parade', an event that
happens every Halloween. It's a casual affair, parents come if
they are able, and it's fun watching the faces of the adorable
children parading in their Halloween getups across the tiny
school yard. I looked around, hoping to catch the eye of a fellow parent so that we might silently share a chuckle. I looked
around, only to be faced with a virtual sea of Steadicams and

Handycams, and other various cams of all shapes and sizes. I did not catch a single eye. In fact, it was difficult to make out any actual faces behind all the lenses. Apparently there was not one parent there who could watch, with his own eyes, his costumed child walk across a small yard, take in the charm of the moment, and treasure the memory forever. Fine, I understand that the spouse couldn't make it and will simply die if she doesn't see a recording of little Fanny walking for twenty feet in her Simba outfit, even though she will see Fanny in her costume tonight when they go out trick-or-treating. But for whom are you really doing this? Who will be the beneficiary of this minutely recorded history? You are denying yourself experiencing the moment, because you think your little Simba will be deprived at some point in the future. You picture her sitting with her fiancé fifteen years hence, watching her tiny self flit across the screen, everybody laughing and watching, and remarking how adorable and skinny everyone was.

This is a disease, and you must be careful not to infect your children with it, or you will raise the type of people who have to see their lives in instant replay, the kind of people who are more intent on recording an event than in creating memories.

This compulsion to record every waking moment of our lives and our children's lives often starts with the birth of the child. Now, I gave birth in a bath, and a dear friend, in between handing me sips of cold juice, apparently took some lovely pictures of the event while I was concentrating on other, more painful things. The photographs are in black-and-white, and I can only be grateful for that, as at the time, I was sitting in water that was growing increasingly red. One doesn't want to see the red. One is blissfully unaware of the red at the time, and one really does not want to be reminded of it at a later date.

I am happy that I have a few beautiful photographs of the birth of my child. Perhaps he will be happy one day to have a memento of his little head popping out of a bath of murky water, along with a few rare commemorative photos of his mother without lipstick or a decent night's sleep. I have no idea what I would do with a videotape of the enchanting event. Watch it with friends? Have a get-together with chilli and party hats, where we all joyfully watch me pop out a baby, in wide-screen splendour?

By all means, bring out the video and DVD cameras once in a while, get some of that family fun down for posterity, but make an effort, now and again, to enjoy the spectacle in real time. Without having to worry about the lighting, or whether your child is in the shot, you may find the show quite entertaining. You may even experience a certain heady feeling of freedom, being unencumbered by cameras, bags, battery packs, and the grave responsibility of recording an important childhood event.

To alleviate occasional pangs of guilt, I have resorted to finding groups of friendly looking parents who are carrying cameras, and claiming, with a distressed look, 'I forgot mine!' One of the sympathetic bunch usually rushes to my aid and offers to take a few snapshots of the event, secretly feeling sorry for my child for having such a bad mummy. I enjoy the show, file the memories away, and usually end up with a couple of souvenir photos that I can stick in the box with all the other loose snapshots that will never be put in a photo album.

CHAPTER 7

NAPPY BAG OR STEAMER TRUNK?

FOR THOSE OF YOU TENTATIVELY ATTEMPTING YOUR FIRST social visits with an infant in tow, try not to frighten your hosts by arriving at their house laden with five overstuffed duffles and a car boot full of baby gear. You are going to visit a friend. You are not going to live in the outback for a month. It is probable that your friends have running water, and unless one is intending a lengthy stay, it is not necessary to pack:

- Ten changes of tiny clothing
- Twenty-five nappies and a jumbo-sized box of wipes
- An entire duffle bag filled with stuffed animals
- A travel cot, with bedding and attached musical-teddy-bears mobile
- A jungle gym
- A bouncy seat, a rocking seat, and a rolling walker
- An entire train set, an inflatable clown, and a drum set
- Several noisemaking, battery-operated toys

Not only will this be alarming to your hosts, it will make you, as parents, feel that it's just Too Much Trouble to go anywhere with your child, and you will slowly end up housebound and friendless.

Most households are sufficiently set up to allow modest food preparation, as well as often having a bed upon which you might change your child and/or lay the infant down for a nap. It is possible to leave your house with nothing but your child and, if you must, a small bag of simple necessities, such as:

- Two to five nappies
- A few plastic bags for disposing of said nappies, and for carrying away the clothes that will no doubt end up covered with some kind of disgusting wet stuff
- A small blanket or two, an extra jumper, a hat
- A small bag full of tiny cars, a colouring book, or reading material, depending on the age of the tot
- A nice bottle of wine for your hosts, which should be opened upon arrival

As for nourishment, if one is nursing an infant, which I would encourage not only for the health of the child but also for the undeniable convenience, one need only bring both breasts, and perhaps a burping cloth, to any occasion. How very modern!

CHAPTER 8

WHEN IT IS TIME TO LEAVE

ONCE YOU'RE READY TO GO, IT'S WISEST NOT TO ASK PERmission of your progeny. Now would not be the time to say, 'Darling, we want to leave in about five minutes, is that okay?' Your child might be having the worst time of his life, but given the opportunity of deciding the fate of the entire family, well, what choice do you think a four-year-old will make?

The slippery slope is all too familiar:

> 'Sweetheart, no more biscuits, we'll be going home for dinner in a few minutes.'
> 'Poppet, I said no more. All right, *one* more, but that's it, because we're leaving! Will you please go and get your backpack?'
> 'Okay, okay, you may have *two* more biscuits, but no whining. Please, sweetie, that's enough. We're leaving. Please put the biscuit down and *please* get your backpack, okay precious?'
> 'Are you ready to go now? I've got your backpack! We're leaving! No more biscuits, darling.'

'Okay, I will let you have one more biscuit in the car, but we're leaving in *two minutes*.'

As the child reluctantly leaves half an hour later, clutching five more biscuits, the chuckling mother exclaims that her little one is 'Such a negotiator! He will probably grow up to be a lawyer!'

No, he will likely grow up to be friendless and unpleasant, and have difficulty functioning in social situations. (He may, in fact, grow up to be a lawyer, perhaps in the entertainment industry, where this type of behaviour is often used to great advantage, but this is a fact of life that should be vigorously withheld from your child's store of knowledge.)

'We are leaving in five minutes' is a good place to start. 'Get your stuff and let's help clean up this mess' is another thoughtful alternative.

When your child finally does depart he really ought to express some gratitude toward his host and hostess. It is an all too familiar experience to have someone's child leave our house without a fare-thee-well after we have fed him, watered him, and indulged him with toys that remain strewn about. We might have even entertained him with a video, or accommodated him on an overnight stay, graciously throwing in a tasty and nutritious breakfast. We say gaily, 'Good-bye! It was so nice to see you!' His mother invariably looks apologetic as her little one races out of the door with hardly a backward glance. She calls out, 'Darling? Darling? Don't you want to say thank you?' No, he really would rather not, now that you ask. With an apologetic look, a tired 'Thank you' is expressed by the mother as she beats a hasty retreat.

Often the mother and father will act as interpreter to their youngster, as if their child is only a visitor in this strange and wonderful country and is still grappling with the language.

'Good-bye!' we cheerfully say to our small departing visitor. 'See you soon!'

Noticing that no actual sounds are coming from the child's mouth, one of the parents hurriedly fills the gap: 'Bye-bye! Bye-bye! Thank you!' the daddy says, with a peculiar lisping quality and in a slightly higher tone of voice than he might normally use. Perhaps Daddy thinks we won't notice that his lips are moving as he lifts his child's tiny hand and waves it at us.

Do not allow your child to grow up to be a social embarrassment. What might have been tolerable, perhaps even adorable, in a child of three or four becomes singularly unpleasant in a child of seven or eight, or twelve. Politeness is always appreciated, and one is never too young or too old to say 'Thank you'.

A Helpful Hint!

ON GETTING OUT OF THE DOOR

AS SOON AS YOUR CHILD IS OLD ENOUGH TO MIMIC YOUR words, teach him by rote some polite and useful phrases. Any of these may be implemented, depending upon the occasion:

> *'Thank you for the lovely party!'*
> *'Thank you for the lovely lunch and nap!'*
> *'Thank you for having me to your house to play!'*
> *'Thank you for your kind hospitality!'*
> *'Thank you for the lovely dinner!'*
> *'Thank you for the lovely time!'*

At two years old he may not be aware of the meaning, but he will receive such wide-eyed adulation and praise that these charming phrases will be burned into his consciousness from an early age. Your child will eventually come to learn what a heartfelt and complimentary farewell will do for the disposition of a tired parent-hostess or -host, and it will soon come to be his second nature.

CHAPTER 9

CHILDREN'S BIRTHDAY PARTIES: NOT JUST FOR CHILDREN!

IN BYGONE DAYS, THE CHILD'S FIRST YEAR WAS CELE-brated with much pomp and festivity, and for good reason: the child had actually survived his first year without succumbing to scurvy, boils, the plague, or any number of those unpleasant childhood illnesses of yore.

I encourage celebrating the first year, and in fact I heartily endorse the celebration of all birthdays. But things have gone completely haywire.

After the age of five, maybe six, your children will possibly begin to retain many magical birthday memories. Before that age, however, it is unlikely that they will remember whether you hired the Methodist Tabernacle Choir to sing 'Happy Birthday' or had your two maiden aunts demonstrate a lively rendition of the Hokey Cokey. Assuming you don't keep them manacled to the radiator, toddlers are generally thrilled by the mere act of living and breathing. Balloons and cake for a birthday celebration are thoughtful, more than necessary, extras.

Although a life-sized Barbie impersonator might be a treat for a few of the daddies, it is probable that your three-year-old will not cherish the memory of a garishly bewigged ex-showgirl practising hackneyed 'magic' tricks on the back patio, or a bitter, marginally employed actor in a Batman cape making balloon animals.

Why not have an afternoon cocktail party? By all means, invite the kids. It's your child's birthday, after all.

If you plan on having more than a few children over to celebrate, hire a local teenager to keep an eye on the tykes while you and the other parents sip chilled alcoholic beverages. If you are fortunate enough to be celebrating a summer birth, well then, turn on the sprinkler and let the naked kiddies loose on the lawn. They may spend hours at this delightful pursuit, and there will be no need for people to exhort them to join in organized activities in which they have no interest. You also have the added benefit of not having to deal with clown-induced nightmares, which can last for weeks.

Lemonade provides refreshment for those too young to appreciate distilled spirits, and the simple addition of a fine vodka creates an easily made and remarkably tasty beverage for an exhausted and grateful grown-up. Don't forget the sprig of fresh mint!

A catered lunch is always appreciated, but certainly not by the children. Eschew the long, gaily papered table and tiny chairs, the forced sitting down to pizza and sandwiches. Children rarely eat at birthday parties, so feed them well beforehand and provide only a bit of sustenance for the few hearty eaters and the peckish parents. Cubes of cheese, crackers, and an icing-laden birthday cake, if you're ambitious.

Devilish Eggs and Weenie Fondue may be enjoyed by the hungrier child or grown-up, and will provide a welcome buffer for the thirsty parent who has taken to the spiked lemonade with a little too much enthusiasm, considering the early hour.

LEMONADE FOR GROWN-UPS

250ml freshly squeezed lemon juice
125g castor sugar (or to taste)
250ml crushed ice
1l water

Place all the ingredients in a jug and mix well, or place in a blender and process until smooth.

Pour into frosty glasses to which you have added:

60ml quality vodka
sprig of crushed mint

Quickly pass to thirsty grown-ups. Omit vodka if serving to the younger set, as it doesn't sit well with them.

WEENIE FONDUE (FOR A CROWD)

30 to 40 hot dogs
4 bottles of HP Chilli Sauce
1 bottle of Marks and Spencer Dijon Mustard
one large container of sour cream
a dash of sweet sherry
a dash of ground pepper
chopped onion, sautéed (optional)

Cook the hot dogs in boiling water for five minutes or so. Cool, and cut into bite-sized chunks. Place the remaining ingredients into a large pot and stir until mixed.

Add the hot dog pieces, as well as sautéed chopped onion, if desired. Warm through, and transfer to your Aunt Ida's old chafing-dish, the one you found in the cellar and thought you'd have no use for.

Serve with toothpicks. Num!

DEVILISH EGGS

2 dozen eggs
100g unsalted butter, softened
120ml mayonnaise, or more to taste
1 tablespoon dried tarragon
60g chopped vermouth-soaked 'drunken' olives
60g minced pickled garlic
salt and pepper
paprika

Bring eggs to a boil, then cover and let sit for 15 minutes off the heat. Plunge eggs in iced water and leave until cool.

Peel the eggs and slice in half lengthwise, popping the yolks into a mixing bowl. Smash yolks together with butter, mayonnaise, tarragon, olives, pickled garlic, and salt and pepper to taste. Cream together until smooth. Place a dollop of the yolk mixture in each egg half, and sprinkle with a pinch of paprika, for colour.

CHAPTER 10

THE FAMILY AT TABLE

WE HAVE ALL SEEN THOSE GLOSSY PHOTO SPREADS IN gourmet food magazines of the joyful yet sophisticated Italian family sitting down to a long table, alfresco, joined by aunts, uncles, and happy wide-eyed youngsters. The children are seemingly enchanted by their watered-down glass of wine, their plates heaped with blood sausage and fava beans. We are led to believe that the adorable Italian children do not pick the garlic and onions out of their food, nor do they bolt from the table after the five minutes it takes them to suck back nine noodles and a baby carrot, leaving you with gaping holes in the well-thought-out alfresco seating arrangement.

Perhaps if we were all Italian, I could gesticulate wildly to my children and bend them to my hot-blooded will, and they would eagerly gobble up plates of succulent *Trippa alle Verdure,* while quietly sipping their faintly pink water. They would listen intently to the worldly grown-ups expounding on affairs of the heart and soul. They would smile, their big, Italian eyes shining, and then they would help serve the gelato.

Perhaps if we were all Italian, the pope would pop out of the *Torta di Vaniglia* and do a fan dance, but we are not Italian, and sometimes the children just have to eat at their own table.

When entertaining guests, feed the youngsters first and they will be well occupied while the grown-ups are having their hors d'oeuvres. They will also enjoy relief from the incessant harangue regarding the crumpled napkin on the table and the noisy licking of fingers. If the weather is fine, send them out of doors to eat, serving a picnic dinner on a blanket, and saving yourself from crumbs on the floor and extra dishes to wash. If the impending snow has you worried about the possibility of frostbitten little fingers and toes, find a room where they can picnic on the floor – preferably a room that can be shut off from the rest of the house. A full meal has the additional benefit of inducing a certain degree of drowsiness in children, which is always a welcome condition when you are dealing with a group of highly strung youngsters.

DON'T FORGET! In cleaning up after an indoor picnic, take extra care to check behind cushions and under sofas for hardened pasta and shriveled bits of carrot, as children often store their food like chipmunks, and can be quite forgetful.

What of the evenings when you are entertaining no one but yourselves? How can one sustain the magic of a shared family meal night after night? Children must eat. Dinner must be prepared with predictable regularity. One attempts to liven up the menu, but there is nothing more disheartening than spending hours in one's kitchen, lovingly preparing a *Tagine Escabeche,* or a hearty *Filet de Boeuf à la Gelée et Tripe,* only to have those in the picky under-five set start poking at their plates and making noise about 'green stuff' in their food.

If you are forced to make dinner for ungrateful children, and you anticipate that their reaction to your *Potaje de Frijoles Blancos con Codornices* will be less than enthusiastic, do not, whatever you do, fall headlong into the 'white food' trap. Do not trot out a plate of wagon-wheel noodles topped with a shake of Parmesan-flavoured cheese product and call it dinner. How in the world are your finicky eaters ever going to raise their level of taste or expand their culinary horizons if they are exposed only to plain noodles and beefburgers? Offer them what the grown-ups are eating. Fill their plates with colour and flavour. If nothing else, they can admire the texture and composition.

It is not your job to spend every evening over a hot stove, preparing two or even three different dinners, catering to every preference in the family. Why not try a novel approach and serve the same dinner to everyone? It may seem difficult at first, getting your children used to this egalitarian plan. They may baulk and make unpleasant faces. They may turn up their noses at Monday evening's braised *Blanquette de Veau* and refuse to eat. Enjoy your meal, and firmly insist that this is what is being served for dinner. On Tuesday night they may rudely refrain from the roasted asparagus ragout, and will almost certainly complain of some vague 'hunger'. Do not be inveigled into whipping up a small pot of macaroni with butter. Wednesday may find them sniffing disdainfully at your *Coq au Poire*, but by Thursday their little tummies will begin to rumble ever so slightly as they glance with longing at the Creole trout puffs. Come Friday, in a weakened and much more malleable state, they will be begging for seconds of spring-pea soup, and clamouring for just one more piece of cauliflower torte.

If you didn't start them on an interesting variety of foods by the time they were a year old, then this method is really the only way to break them of their pernickety eating habits. As long as they are given plenty of fresh water to drink, they shouldn't be in any serious danger.

Attempt to avoid the ubiquitous 'negotiating' that goes on at dinner tables across the country, which is really nothing more than bribing children to eat dinner.

They poke at their salad, they move the carrots and broccoli around the plate. You propose a deal: In exchange for taking 'just five more big bites' they can have sweets beyond their wildest dreams. 'Just three more bites' will get them biscuits and ice cream. The child puts two grains of rice into his mouth and demands dessert. You will be exhausted, and your child will get dessert, having won the battle. So it will go, meal after meal, night after night.

If you must try to reason with them, do not barter with food. Use a cherished nonfood item as a bargaining chip, for instance telling them they will not get to watch their favourite video or play poker after dinner unless they eat all of their vegetables. Dessert is taken out of the equation. Simple. Clean. They keep up their end, you keep up yours.

Bon appétit!

ON HAVING YOUR COOKING APPRECIATED

I HAVE FOUND A WONDERFUL SOLUTION THAT WILL GUAR-antee you get at least a few hours a week of healthy, enthusiastic praise for your cooking: cultivate the friendship of a bachelor. A young couple will sometimes do, but a bachelor is really best, preferably a bachelor whom your spouse finds enjoyable as well. Irish bachelors are ideal, as they are unfailingly polite even after having polished off a third of the Jameson's, and they are often eccentric, which makes them wonderful dining companions. An eccentric Irish bachelor will also provide your children with a questionable role model, which is really the best kind.

Plan on having your new bachelor friend over for dinner on a regular basis, maybe once a week, as this will afford you the opportunity to try out many new and exotic dishes to which your family might, under more private circumstances, turn up their noses. The addition of 'company' at the dinner table deters one's spouse from making annoyed faces at the braised kale with lemon and olives, and the effusive expressions of appreciation you will receive from your Irish bachelor will give you the will to endure wrinkled noses for the rest of the week. Your bachelor may ask for seconds, and even thirds. He will ask of your spouse, 'Do you always get to eat this well?' in that beguiling lilt. He will ooh and aah, and eagerly gobble up whatever you put in front of him. It is most gratifying.

CHAPTER 11

CHILD LABOUR:
NOT JUST FOR THE THIRD WORLD!

IT WAS NOT THAT LONG AGO THAT CHILDREN WERE brought into this world for the sole purpose of keeping up the family farm. Women with serviceable hips and calloused hands popped out legions of boy and girl farmhands, who were required, at an early age, to rise at ungodly hours in order to milk cows or goats, to dig ditches, and to split firewood.

The demands of a small household in an urban environment may not be quite so great, but I say it is high time we realize that we have a wealth of energetic and affordable labour sitting in front of the television set snacking on overpriced novelty foods. Let's tap this underutilized national resource, for the sake of their characters, and because we can.

Most children love the sound of a vacuum cleaner, and their size makes them ideal for reaching those tight, hard-to-get-at spots. Three years old is not too soon to start learning the fundamentals of decent vacuuming.

Clearing the table of dishes is another excellent task to which you might set your child. Honestly, is there anything more endearing than the sight of small-statured persons whisking away the dirty dishes at a dinner party, especially when one can't quite afford the diminutive foreign help one so longs for? If you are worried about those in the under-five set handling the Limoges, I suggest using colourful plastic dinnerware. Vintage melamine is a chic choice for a festive dining experience, and children may stack the plates with no fear of breakage.

Polishing silver is a satisfying chore for any youngster, as are polishing furniture and washing windows. Compliment your child's work and encourage thoroughness, reminding him that if he lived in Pakistan or Turkey he would be hunkered over a loom for nine hours a day, or busy hand knotting rugs in a very stuffy room. You might also consider giving him a small fee for his hard work, using the occasion to rid your coin purse of all those extra pennies. Ten pence is a fortune to a four-year-old, and is certainly more than he'd be getting after a hard day in Sri Lanka sewing corporate insignias on baseball caps.

Children are prone to rising all too early in the morning, with seemingly nothing to do but call for Mummy to pour them some cereal, and cut them an apple, and turn on the video machine. Well, sometimes Mummy has had a hard night, and sometimes Mummy needs a tiny bit of extra sleep, and perhaps just a few aspirin.

There is no reason why you can't pour your child's favourite cereal into a bowl the night before, placing it within easy reach of the tiny tot. Leaving some milk in a little jug on a lower shelf of the refrigerator would be the thoughtful thing to do, but if you are afraid of spillage, I suggest extolling the virtues of dry cereal for breakfast. If your child is older than, say, four, there is no reason on earth why he shouldn't be getting his own breakfast, and picking the paper up from the front lawn while he's at it.

A child who has never been given chores to do is a child who grows up with a skewed sense of entitlement. He shares your home but, strangely, things get picked up after him. The bedsheets are magically changed and laundered, the dinner table is miraculously set every night, and he is rarely told to lift a finger to clean up his messes. It's just easier to do everything yourself, so he never learns how food gets from the super-market to his plate. He is never asked to water the garden, or help weed the flower beds, or find the caterpillars on your tomatoes, because he doesn't seem interested, or you have a gardener who comes anyway. The washing machine is a mys-tery, and folding clothes is something that is apparently done by the clothes-folding fairy. If this is still a portrait of your child at age seven or eight or nine, then you are overdue in introducing your little one to the stimulating world of house-hold chores.

It is time for you to get some much deserved help around the house, not only to lighten your work-load but to save your child from growing into an arrogant and spoiled teenager and, ultimately, a helpless grown-up.

FISCAL PLANNING AND YOUR TOOTH FAIRY

LITTLE SASHA BOASTS TO HER KINDERGARTEN CLASSMATES *during break that the tooth fairy left twenty pounds under her pillow. That was the tooth fairy at her dad's house; the tooth fairy at her mum's only left her ten pence. Parents, can we all get together on this tooth fairy business? I know some of you may have wads of extra twenties just burning a hole in that mattress, but please, save yourself a few pounds, and let the rest of us off the hook. I realize we must adjust for inflation, and the old rules of ten pence per tooth and twenty pence for a molar no longer apply, but twenty pounds? Are you mad? Your child is five. What will she be expecting when she is nine?*

I suggest you follow the lead of our tooth fairy, who knows that there is no real magic in a used five pound note, much less a twenty. This particular, very clever tooth fairy leaves the children a fifty pence piece for every regular tooth they lose, and a gold sovereign for every molar. The heavy feel of the coins thrills the children much more than cheap, paper money, and it's not difficult to convince them that they are collecting rare and valuable gold ingots, available only in the enchanted land where the tooth fairy dwells. This fiction is simple to perpetuate, as these coins are rarely circulated; children generally know their pounds and pence fairly early in life, but the giant gold coinage turning up under their pillows can only be from some other, much more interesting world.

CHAPTER 12

AVOIDING THE DETRITUS
OF CHILDHOOD

YOUR LITTLE ONE IS GETTING BIGGER, AND ALONG WITH the growth of your youngster come more, and bigger, toys. How many times have we visited a friend's heretofore neat and sparkling house only to find every room turned into her child's own personal playground? Is it necessary that the areas frequented by grown-ups be set up like an obstacle course, seemingly for the sole purpose of causing bodily injury to those grown-ups who wear either bifocals or high heels or both? Is it a given that your house become a receptacle for every manner of plastic dump truck and cheap nylon tunnelling system? There are many things one can do to avoid this pitfall.

The first thing that comes to mind is not to start collecting so many toys in the first place. When your child is very, very young, cultivate the friendship of other people who have children. Then, go over to their houses and have your child play with *their* toys. Single first-time parents, especially those who have recently been through a messy divorce, are an ideal choice, as not only do they go to town when it comes to buying paraphernalia for their little bundle, but you will be able to choose between two separate houses full of staggering examples of one-upmanship between the former spouses. The toys are generally new and shiny, and whole rooms are often devoted to the lavish entertainment of their cherished offspring. In addition, these children are usually less protective of, and more generous with, their toys, as they have two sets of everything. Your child will receive all of the benefit, while you bear none of the annoyance of having to store giant plastic indoor slide sets and an entire fleet of midget-sized earth-moving equipment.

As your child begins to notice that there are not a lot of things to play with in his own house, introduce the concept of small toys. Small is intriguing. Small is nifty. Small is savvy! Many, many good things come in small packages, and all are put away easily and neatly at the end of the day. Assign a drawer or two in a fabulous piece of furniture for the storage of these tiny treasures. Your living room will retain the look of a grown-up place of rest and revelry, while cleverly hiding a wealth of kiddie entertainment. Extol the virtues of all things miniature, and encourage your child to help you find unique 'hiding' places for his delightful little playthings. Tiny cars can be purchased for next to nothing, whole sets can be had for the price of a couple of double lattes, and hours of play will be enjoyed by your child, while you attend to your tasks.

If a handful of these tiny cars should not make it back to their storage area, simply display them on the mantelpiece, as most of them are cunningly designed and really quite chic. Be sure to get the Matchbox James Bond Aston Martin, with the ejector seat, which will fill your male adult guests with sentimental longing. Use them as place-card holders at your next dinner party, or give them as parting gifts to your adult guests, who will be terribly charmed by your whimsy. At this point you will have accumulated so many cars that your child is not likely to miss ten or fifteen of them.

I also cannot say enough about the marvellous trend of having 'micro' versions of all the action heroes. You can actually purchase entire sets of action figures, including their spaceships, automobiles, and helicopters, that are roughly the size of fingernail parings. These are adorable and exceedingly diminutive toys. They will never clutter up a room, as they will usually be buried in the half-inch pile of your living room carpet. When they are finally found, they may be comfortably housed in one of your empty cigarette boxes.

A NOTE TO THOSE PARENTS WHO LIVE IN FLATS IN LARGE METROPOLITAN AREAS: when tiny friends pop over to play with your child, you are not in a position to send them out of doors, as you have no garden available nor really any greenery. Simply move a few potted plants onto a balcony to create an enchanting jungle effect and provide an excellent backdrop for small action figures and cars. It may be necessary to warn the porter below to watch for airborne toys, but the children will be out of your hair, playing happily in the fresh air, and your flat will remain surprisingly neat.

CHAPTER 13

NURSERY: THE FAST TRACK
TO OXFORD

AT A DINNER PARTY ONE EVENING, I FOUND MYSELF IN conversation with another parent of a preschooler. This man was a lawyer, and had grown up in one of those lovely small towns somewhere in the middle part of the country, where they have bucolic scenery, ponds, woods, and real fires in winter. I asked this man if he ever thought about moving back to his hometown with the family to bring up his child away from the smog and congestion of a large city. He replied that he had thought about it, but that he didn't want to jeopardize his son's 'future earning potential'.

His child was four years old. Four. Years. Old.

Future. Earning. Potential.

Another couple I know have put their darling ten-month-old on a waiting list for a nursery school they recently visited. They sincerely love the atmosphere of the place, but are worried that the academics might be a little lax.

Nursery. Academics.

I'm not advocating that you encourage stupidity in your offspring, although a simple child is certainly simpler to cope with, but I would suggest you think long and hard before popping in the *Baby Einstein* tape. A bright child is to be hoped for; a really intelligent one can be time-consuming and often rather repellent.

For instance, you may have never considered the downside of having an early reader. While you may pat yourself on the back for all the time you have put in with the flashcards and educational computer games, driving in the car with your toddler will more quickly become a living nightmare, as he is now able to read the words 'Toy Shop', 'Sweets', 'Funtime Video Arcade', and, of course, 'Live Nude Girls'.

True, less of your precious time is required to read aloud to your four-year-old since she discovered the classics, and you are only occasionally needed to explain the meaning of certain obscure literary or historical references. However, all that extra time on your hands must now be devoted to transporting your gifted and talented child to all those gifted and talented after-school and weekend activities. Personally, I have worked long and hard for my Saturday sleep-in. If you can find a nice violin teacher within walking distance, then fine, let your little daughter wake up at some ungodly hour, pack up her baby Stradivarius, and walk to her lesson. I'm sure she'll happily practise for an hour every morning, too, and perhaps solve the riddle of Fermat's Last Theorem in time for lunch. Just let me sleep.

The most compelling argument against having highly intelligent children is the fact that they will all too soon become

acutely aware of how bright they are and, consequently, how stupid you are. It will begin with the incessant questions, which they will eventually discover leave you as much in the dark as they. This will soon lead them to question your intellect and, ultimately, your authority. It does no good to explain that you, yourself, are sadly a victim of a poor elementary educational system, and that in addition, you don't know where Azerbaijan is because when you were ten years old there *was* no Azerbaijan. Quickly ask them to point to Constantinople on the map, and then say 'Aha! My point exactly.' This may buy you some time, but pretty soon Mr or Miss Smarty-Pants will find you out, and it will be the end of your role as an effective parent. And on a practical note, having a child of average intelligence will help you avoid unnecessary and costly hospital bills, as he is much less likely to be beaten to a pulp after school than the child who possesses an overweening aptitude.

Of course, highly intelligent girls tend to stay away from dating until they are at university, which is rather a good thing, and certainly you will save time and money not shopping for and purchasing various silly outfits, but all in all, the easiest type of child to have underfoot is the kind, affectionate, independent, simple child. The type of child who won't lose sleep if he doesn't excel at his kindergarten interview.

CHAPTER 14

THE THREE-MARTINI PLAYDATE

I REALIZE THAT THE DAYS MAY BE OVER WHEN A MOTHER could send her five-year-old through the door with a cheerful 'Be back in time for dinner!', secure in the knowledge that her little one would wander over to some friendly neighbour's house and get in the hair of that friendly neighbour for a while. Those days were not only good for the mothers, they were good for the inquisitive young child, who could learn the geography of the area, observe unfamiliar people in their habitats, and occasionally get accidentally locked in some interesting neighbour's bathroom. A child could ask endless questions of an adult other than his parent, an adult who might find him enchanting, an adult who might think it a real treat to have him over for a chat and possibly a biscuit. A child could run over to the Worcesters' to play 'house' with the Worcester girls, or up to the Breezebottoms to play 'doctor' with little Stevie, or out into the middle of the street to play 'I spy' until it was time to come in for dinner.

In these modern times, we have the playdate. One must schedule one's child for a *date* to *play* with another child, usually because the child likes playing with your child at nursery, and they think they can re-create the magic in a domestic setting. Sometimes he simply wants to see what kind of toys your child has been stockpiling, or he would like to show your child his own recent acquisitions.

Occasionally my husband and I find that we actually like the child, and we hope that the parents are tolerable, as we will be forced to sit in their house making interminable small talk while the children play. More often than not, we find we have nothing in common with these people, that they have invited us only because their sweet picklepuss wants our child to come over. Perhaps they are attempting to socialize their ill-behaved offspring by surrounding him with lots and lots of nice boys and girls, and are willing to hobnob with total strangers to accomplish this formidable task. The situation is frequently as awkward as a bad blind date, and one must endure a forced, often painful chat, attempting to answer such questions as 'So, what do you *do*?' while discussing the ins and outs of early childhood development. Aside from simply declining every invitation and being thought of as an unpleasant recluse who keeps one's child a virtual prisoner, these playdates must be reciprocated, and you will, sooner or later, be expected to sacrifice some otherwise fine and relaxing afternoons to entertaining a succession of people with whom you have no shared interests other than the fact that your children like to play together.

In the spirit of *The Philadelphia Story* or the *Addams Family*, when forced to entertain dull or insufferable fellow parents, show off your home milieu in the most eccentric possible light. Answer the door in an orange kaftan, a cigarette dangling from a long, ivory-handled holder. If you are a nonsmoker, those fake herbal cigarettes that smell like burning hair are equally effective. Invite assorted 'arty' types to visit 'unexpectedly'. Encourage your musician friend to swing by with his accordion. Talk about how much you are repelled by the word and the very concept of the playdate, and as a last resort, bring up a controversial political or religious topic.

If your child plays well with this particular girl or boy but you really cannot bear to sit with the parent and discuss crafts projects for the nursery one more time, suggest that the parent leave the child and come back in a few hours, giving assurances that you'll feed the kids a nutritious snack and watch them like a hawk. Try not to make the suggestion sound as if you find this parent the most dull conversationalist in the world and you really wish she would vacate the premises before your face cracks and you throw an ashtray through the window. Make it sound as if you want to give her the opportunity to get a few errands done or browse at the bookshop, and one day she may gratefully pay you back in kind. Chances are, if you are uncomfortable, she is too, and will eagerly take you up on the offer.

If you simply don't have the energy to parade various unsavoury artistic types or the heart to play your entire collection of Engelbert Humperdinck on vinyl, I have discovered an easy and fun solution for quickly weeding out the types of parents with whom you would rather not share your afternoons. When forced into a playdate situation, invite the parents over around the cocktail hour. The cocktail hour may be an hour, more or less, around four o'clock, at which time I suggest you noisily and with much gusto mix up a batch of cold martinis. This is a surefire method of separating the wheat from the chaff, the cream from the nondairy soya alternative. If, after you have offered drinks all around, the visiting parents quickly gather the child and child-related paraphernalia and run silently from your house, enjoy your martini with the knowledge that these people were not the sort with whom you would want to embark upon a long-term playdate relationship. If, however, their eyes light up and sighs of relief can be heard (as well as faintly audible whimpering noises), you may have the beginning of a workable alliance.

Difficulties occasionally arise when you do end up becoming fast friends with a child's parents only to discover later that their spawn is a horrid brat who torments your child regularly, and whom your child cannot abide. Suggest to these unfortunate people that you all get baby-sitters and have an adult evening out. Enjoy yourselves while you can, as this type of adult relationship usually does not last long, unless their child grows out of his psychotic tendencies in a hurry.

Once in a blue moon there is a happy confluence, and the best of all situations is achieved: a kind, thoughtful, and interesting child, blessed with parents of the same bent. You think they're terrific and, oddly enough, they seem to think the same of you. When one stumbles upon this ideal combination, relish it, and celebrate. Keep plenty of olives and ice on hand and have them over often. For a playdate.

- CHAPTER 15 -

MUMMY, I WANT A PUPPY!

NO, YOU DON'T. UNLESS YOU ARE TRULY A DOG PERSON, have always kept dogs and cared for them, unless you happily run them at six a.m. and lovingly clean up the hardened logs of poo that dot the landscape of your back lawn, unless you chuckle at the sight of chewed Italian nubuck and enjoy carrying plastic bags full of faecal waste when you're out on a little walk, unless you are used to doing all these things and more, do not be swayed by the plaintive and repeated requests from your son or daughter for a canine companion.

Neither should you, against your better judgement, adopt a fluffy little kitten just because darling Tiffany pleaded with her limpid eyes and promised to take care of it 'fowever and ever'. You know full well that it is only a matter of weeks before that adorable, fluffy little furball becomes a lean and lanky cat, losing all its appeal to anyone other than elderly house-bound ladies and people who collect unicorn figurines. You will have nothing but coughed-up hairballs on the sofa and an arrogant, furry houseguest that will shun your company, shred your furniture, and laugh at you behind your back for being such a sucker. Yes, cats laugh. At you.

If your child insists on hounding you to buy a pet, and should you find yourself on the verge of giving in, do yourself a favour and start small. A fish is generally a good bet, as long as you don't lose all professional control and end up with a sixty-gallon tank that you will have to empty and clean every other week, with no help from anyone. No, what you want is a goldfish, the kind that comes in a plastic bag full of water, the kind you place in a small fishbowl with a quivering stem of greenery, the kind that will die.

When your goldfish dies – and it will die rather quickly – do not be tempted to rush out and buy a doppelgänger goldfish. You may fool your child and avoid some unpleasantness, but you will be missing out on a wonderful opportunity for a frank discussion regarding the brief flame of life, the shadow of death, and the senselessness of keeping living creatures in cramped quarters. If you should want to accelerate the whole process, place your goldfish in the classic fishbowl with a piece of *plastic* seaweed rather than the real thing. The plastic seaweed – and it must have been manufactured for this purpose; why else would they sell it? – will add no actual oxygen to the small habitat, and you will be able to witness your own private Circle of Life in short order.

Let your children see Spot or Fred white-belly up in the fishbowl. Discuss funerary options. Burial at sea? Open coffin? Satin-lined, or a cheap cardboard model? While it may be an uncomfortable discussion for your young ones, it will aid immeasurably in souring them on the idea of ever having a pet again. Have a little burial ceremony, or perhaps a cremation, which could turn into a valuable lesson in land usage and the environment.

If this little episode does not put them off the idea of keeping pets, or if they insist on having another go with the fish, suggest Sea-Monkeys instead! Although nearly microscopic, Sea-Monkeys exude the aura of mythical ocean creatures, making them much more interesting than the common goldfish. Sea-Monkeys require very little care, arrive in their own self-contained unit, and always provide a good conversation starter when guests come to call. Just add water! The hours fly by in the happy pursuit of simply trying to see them.

A WORD OF CAUTION: After your wee ones are tucked in for the night, you may find some of your adult guests passing around the Sea-Monkey habitat in an effort to reclaim some of the Sea-Monkey magic of their youth. This is the cause of many a Sea-Monkey accident, and care should be taken that the Sea-Monkeys are not carelessly spilled on the lap of an enthusiastic partygoer. It will appear that ordinary tap water has

soaked his khakis, but it is highly disconcerting for your guest, who will be acutely aware that a colony of Sea-Monkeys has lodged in his nether regions.

Should such an accident occur, you might be tempted simply to fill the container back up with tap water and avoid eye contact with your child for a day or two. Come clean. Your children will know. There is no hiding a spillage of Sea-Monkeys from children, as they are the only people who can actually see them.

Other 'Pet' Options You Will Want to Avoid:
Snakes. Some children are intrigued by the idea of keeping a snake as a pet. Snakes are certainly fascinating creatures, but much more so when viewed in their natural habitat, or behind glass at the zoo's Snake House. Snakes require either fresh or frozen mice in order to survive. A fresh mouse does not mean a mouse that has been quietly dispatched by some skilled pet shop employee; it means you will be placing a live, furry, squeaking mouse into the tank with the snake, settling in with your child, and perhaps a bag of popcorn, to witness nature taking its inevitable course.

As an alternative, one may actually purchase frozen mice embryos to nourish one's snake. The sight of a snake viciously attacking a frozen mouse embryo is a sad one indeed, and although the box of frozen mice embryos features an adorable cartoon of ice-skating mice wearing tiny hats and scarves, be warned that the actual embryos do not look anywhere near as jubilant as they are depicted on the box.

Lizards. If you keep your lizards in the house, you will be required to bring crickets into your house, to feed the lizards. Crickets. Into the house. Crickets make a charming kind of chirping sound when heard outside, perhaps around a campfire, at night. When you bring them indoors, and they escape from the lizard tank, and they build a massive colony of nests and tunnels in your attic that would rival the Roman catacombs, their chirping will drive you slowly insane. In addition, it's bad luck to kill them.

Turtles. A turtle is not a pet, it is a sculpture. A slowly moving sculpture. Turtles are the Japanese performance artists of the reptile world.

Rodents. Rats have no business indoors, and as for hamsters, there is nothing more hellish than the sound of that squeaking wheel, spinning, all night long, as the small, deranged creature endlessly chases nothing, the persistent whine of the wheel simply a noisy reminder of the futility of our own lives. A guinea pig is similarly pathetic, as well as looking more like a fashionable chapeau than a pet.

A NOTE ON FERRETS: Do not let any whimsical individual sell you on the idea that letting loose a pack of ferrets into a living room full of four-year-olds will be an enchanting birthday surprise. Ferrets are the slinking, hyperactive keepers to the gates of purgatory, and are capable of inducing night terrors in even the hardiest of grown-ups. On the other hand, this may be precisely the effect you are looking for, if you are hoping to end the party on the early side, and put closure on the whole concept of pets.

CHAPTER 16

'CHILDREN'S MUSIC': WHY?

PEOPLE GROWING UP BEFORE THE ADVENT OF *SESAME Street* were denied the pleasures of *Babysongs,* Raffi's greatest hits, and Barney's blatantly appropriated 'This Old Man'. Somehow we all worked out 'I love you, you love me', and that we are a happy fam-i-ly without having it drummed into our heads by an annoying purple dinosaur. My personal musical exposure was varied. Occasionally my father would sing something about the moon, in Japanese, which was highly entertaining to me and my sisters, probably because our father is not, in fact, Japanese. I often remember falling asleep to the sounds of 'Moonlight Sonata' being played on the piano (all but that irksome third movement). A small record collection filled out much of my musical education, and as I grew I happily discovered Billie Holiday, Spike Jones, and the piano artistry of Jonathan Edwards and his two left hands. My performing repertoire consisted of 'Chopsticks' for the piano and 'Ninety-nine Green Bottles hanging on the Wall' for long trips in the car.

There are millions of fine pieces of music from which to choose without a parent having to resort to children's CDs or tapes rife with lifeless and irritating children's music. Fill the house with sound and don't be afraid of listening to the kind of audio entertainment you prefer. Of course, if your tastes run exclusively to playing your favourite Led Zeppelin album from high school on a continual loop, then by all means use your child as an excuse to infuse new life into your listening library.

As predictably as the sun rises each morning, however, your little one will want to listen to one piece of music over and over and over again. It must be played every time you go somewhere in the car, and as often as possible at home. It is a bizarre trait in most children under the age of six, and all the more reason to introduce him to a piece of music that *you* will enjoy as much the five hundredth time you hear it as you did the first.

Perhaps worse than the most insipid children's song is the children's song with a Moral. These songs are put on music and videotapes with the sole purpose of brainwashing our youngsters.

What's wrong with songs telling kids how much fun it is to brush their teeth and how nice it is to share? Well, in the abstract, nothing. The messages are innocuous enough, but you are introducing your children to prosaic, overly literal lyrics, coupled with dispirited, mostly lousy music. If you are preparing them for a lifetime of listening to Top 40 chart hits, then you will have given them the perfect start, as they will develop no discernible musical taste.

But there is also a very real mental health danger to bad music that is rarely mentioned: the melody and lyrics will get stuck on a continual loop in one's head, often for weeks at a time. Your child will be humming the tune under his breath at all hours of the day, and you will absentmindedly sing it while making coffee in the morning. What little sanity you had left will slowly crumble; you will soon find yourself making smiley-faced pancakes, collecting colourfully costumed teddy bears, and decorating with plaid. You will begin to think that mother-daughter matching outfits are *really sweet!* Your friends will no longer drop by, because you offer them healthy fruit snacks instead of a glass of wine, and they have to hear about all the funny things your child said. Avoid bad music and you avoid an insidious and downward descent into sheer blandness.

FOR YOUR LISTENING PLEASURE

BELOW IS A SHORT AND COMPLETELY SUBJECTIVE PLAYLIST of songs and musical selections that may help you in your attempt to avoid the brain-numbing effects of children's music; these pieces may be enjoyed by both children and adults alike.

Bizet's **Carmen.** *Explain that* chien *means 'dog' in French and why Carmen uses such a pejorative to her lover, and your children will not care that this is opera and sung in a foreign language.*

The Boswell Sisters singing anything. Three-part harmony by a trio of sisters from New Orleans, recorded between 1925 and 1932. Learn all the words to 'Nights When I Am Lonely' and 'Crazy People'. Tell your children that they're listening to singing mice.

The Beatles. Start with a viewing of A Hard Day's Night, *the original music video. Playing the cassette in the car guarantees that you soon will have a young Beatles fan on your hands. Help!* is a good follow-up, but save Sgt. Pepper *and the* White Album *for the teenage years.*

XTC. More pop, beloved by kids under five and over ten, as well as their parents.

How the World Wags *by the City Waites, including an actual seventeenth-century farting song. Who can resist?*

Django Reinhardt and Le Hot Club of France. Hot rhythms, played by a fascinating three-fingered gypsy guitarist.

Bluegrass and old-time Cajun music are both very danceable, and often involve accordions. You cannot go wrong with accordions.

Spike Jones. 'Cocktails for Two'. 'Laura'. Whee!!

Musicals. Put on the rousing 'Oh, What a Beautiful Morning' as you make school lunches, mambo across the floor to the West Side Story *prologue, serve breakfast to 'Food, Glorious, Food', from* Oliver! *Do a living room fan waltz to 'I Could Have Danced All Night', swoon to* The Music Man's *'Goodnight, My Someone'. If you start these exercises while they are still young, your children won't laugh at you as they get older. Sadly, some fathers find the prospect of their male children listening to selections from the musical theatre particularly alarming. Relax. Recent advances* in science assure us that a steady diet of Rodgers and Hammerstein will not suddenly turn your son gay. In any event, you will have at least done your part to assure that he's a hit at parties.

DON'T FORGET Mozart, Bach, Beethoven, symphonies, partitas, and sonatas. Debussy, Vivaldi, Renata Tebaldi, The Bobs, Cab Calloway, Aretha, Jackie Wilson, and Al Green. And, bending my own rules, Peter, Paul and Mary. If you haven't sung 'Puff the Magic Dragon' with your child yet, go outside tonight, build a little campfire in the garden, toast some marshmallows, and sing 'Puff the Magic Dragon' together. Cry. When the firemen arrive, they will most likely overlook the bonfire and be happy to add their manly voices to the chorus.

CHAPTER 17

ARE WE THERE YET?
ON THE ROAD WITH MAX
AND MADDY

A CROSS-COUNTRY MARATHON MIGHT NOT BE THE BEST choice for those attempting their first road trip with kiddies in tow, but with a bit of preparation, an expedition can be an exciting, educational, and fun adventure for you and your family. Though hitting the road with two children under the age of ten in the backseat may not exactly evoke the image of Jack Kerouac wending his way through the heartland, or of Thelma and Louise careening through the desert in a red convertible, one mustn't overlook the undeniable pleasure of greeting each day in a brand-new location, with no dishes to wash.

Travelling light is important, so that there's no luggage under your feet in the car and less to carry when you arrive, but one must take into consideration certain essentials. If your four-year-old will be despondent without her scruffy little sock monkey, then you mustn't leave the sock monkey on the kitchen counter, or think that this would be the ideal time to accidentally throw the sock monkey into the rubbish bin. Let your little one pack a small – very small – backpack or duffel full of the small toys or action figures that will help her get through the day. Nothing is worse than a four-year-old in the backseat with the DT's because she is going through stuffed-bunny withdrawal.

Spending the night before the trip packing the bags with the youngsters not only adds excitement to the anticipation of travel, but also should work in your favour the next day, especially if you keep them up hours past their usual bedtime, folding the clothes 'just so'. Sleepy travellers are often the best travellers, as once they get past the initial moody phase, they will often provide you with hours of blessed silence. It is surprising how long a child will sleep in a moving vehicle, and if the weather is warm and the conversation monotonous enough, they will often drop off rather quickly.

Discuss financial-planning strategies with your adult travelling companion, or have your sport-minded spouse explain the finer points of the cricket bowling averages, giving a detailed description of the first day of the last Test. Any discussion of golf is also a guaranteed soporific, and your little one should be down by the second hole. If the moody phase seems to be going on longer than you can bear, consider creating your own warm-weather conditions by turning up the heat in the car. A drowsy state is immediately achieved, and dozing cannot be far behind. Be sure to crack the driver's window if you are concerned about nodding off at the wheel. If you are not the driver for this leg of the journey, ask to hear all about the next three holes of the golf game, and have a little snooze yourself. You've earned it!

It will be tempting to stop for some grub, to use the road-side vernacular, at a familiar-looking chain restaurant. You are far from home and you think the children might feel more comfortable, or you are under some misguided impression that these places are 'cleaner', or the food is 'safer'. Snap out of it. You are on the road. Choose adventure! Find a greasy spoon cafe, the kind that displays a sign outside exclaiming CHILDREN, DOGS AND SOCIAL MISFITS WELCOME! or some similarly charming sentiment. These establishments usually have a 'trucker' section, which is as fascinating to the adults as it is to the children. Beefy, red-faced men in plaid shirts sit in their own little roped-off VIP area, before plates of bacon cheeseburgers and chips, ribbing the waitresses in a familiar manner. The waitresses, many of whom sport unusually large hairdos, will either look at you with beady-eyed suspicion or call you 'luv'. Or both! Do not expect to find any organic leaves in your house salad; in fact, do not expect to find a house salad at all. Enjoy a nice All Day Breakfast. With chips. You are on holiday, for heaven's sake.

The cashier's station usually carries everything from minia-ture Beanie Babies to WD-40. This is where you should purchase an inexpensive trinket for your child, perhaps a small tanker truck or a souvenir postcard. If your children are used to living in a major metropolitan area, it will be an eye-opening introduction to the Rest of the Country, a country with which they may be quite unfamiliar. Instruct your children not to stare at all the white people with crew cuts.

If your child is the kind of traveller who insists he needs to pee every twenty minutes while on the road, forcing you to stop yet again at some godforsaken petrol station or cafe, understand that he is only engaging in a simple power struggle. He is strapped in a car seat, or a seat belt. He believes that he's uncomfortable. He has no control over the vehicle or the radio. The initial excitement of the open road has rapidly faded. He wants out. His instinct tells him that you would be less than pleased over the prospect of driving for three more hours with the scent of a urine-soaked car seat, so he tells you he *has to pee now!* If this begins to happen every fifteen to twenty minutes, simply pull the car over to the side of the road. Regale your child with stories of how when *you* were a child, service stations were few and far between, and peeing by the roadside was a rite of passage. Make the stop as uncomfortable as possible, perhaps by a hedge of brambles, or by an abandoned and derelict water treatment plant. When your child realizes that penny chews and sanitary toilet-seat covers are no longer within whining distance, a strong bladder will begin to develop, and with it, a much more enjoyable trip for everyone.

Bon voyage!

ENTERTAINMENT ON THE ROAD

'COUNTING' GAMES ARE EASY AND FUN, SHOULD THE SCENERY cease to engage your child's interest. Counting Cows is always a treat on stretches of rural road, as are these other games.

- *Counting Foreign Number Plates*
- *Counting Cars That Aren't Four Wheel Drive Jeeps*
- *Counting Drivers Talking on Mobile Phones*
- *Counting Foreign Plates on Cars That Aren't Jeeps (Double points!)*
- *Counting Speeding Red Sports Cars*
- *Counting Highway Patrolmen Hiding in the Bushes with a Radar Gun (Triple points!)*

Making up songs will pass the time in a quite enjoyable manner. Use the tried-and-true 'sung to the tune of' approach to aid you in your musical efforts.

- *Make up songs about farmyard animals and the sounds they make.*

- *Make up songs about small people driving inappropriately large four wheel drive vehicles.*
- *Make up songs about hated teachers or school administrators, and the sounds they make.*
- *Make up new, more gruesome verses to 'Found a Peanut'.*

'Story' is an always entertaining game, where the prisoners of the backseat make up stories about the people they see in passing cars or by the side of the road. Are they aliens? Government spies? How did they get there, and what are they doing? Attempt to outdo one another either in elaborate details or subtlety of description.

A WORD OF CAUTION for those travelling with two or more children: engaging in road games might provide a temporary diversion, but the situation can deteriorate rather quickly into violence, or at the very least disagreeable bickering over who saw what first, or who has counted more VW Beetles. If you are travelling with teens, special dispensation may be allowed for them to have headphones and a CD apparatus, as it may prevent them from torturing or maiming their younger siblings.

Do not take this as a directive to fill the back seat with hand-held electronic game devices. A certain amount of boredom is *necessary for a child's development, and will eventually spark a mental state known as 'daydreaming'. This is a state of mind with which your youngster may be quite unfamiliar, if he spends his days with his eyes glued to hand-held electronic games; a state of mind that is quite pleasurable, in addition to aiding in the growth of the 'imagination'. Suggest that he stare out of the window or mentally join the dots in the car upholstery. Many of the world's problems are solved in just this manner. (Pack a few extra puzzle books just in case.)*

CHAPTER 18

SCHOOL DAYS, SCHOOL DAYS

SUDDENLY THAT DAY IS UPON US. THAT HAPPY DAY WHEN your youngster finally makes her first real foray out of the nest. Kindergarten. You drop her off early in the morning, give her a big hug, and know that she is happily ensconced in educational and fulfilling activities until you fetch her sometime around three o'clock. The school does their job, and you do yours.

Not anymore. Now that your little one is in school, be prepared to be as involved as if you yourself were back sitting at a tiny desk, dipping your fingers into pots of glue and paint. All schools these days, state or private, expect a hearty level of participation from one or both parents. When you are not helping your child through the three hours of homework every night, you will be hauling rocks or counting book forms or writing grants.

For some reason, paying ten thousand pounds a year for kindergarten does not buy you an exemption from making crafts or landscaping the little garden. Nor does it mean that you aren't expected to fork over another chunk of change for each fundraising activity.

Providing that little extra when your child attends a state school, however, is often very gratifying, and usually means the difference between having extra teacher's aides, a few new books, and the occasional music class. (The choice between a state school and an overpriced institution for learning is a personal choice, however, a choice I will leave to you. Far be it from me to judge if you should choose to pay a breath-taking amount of money so that your child might be sur-rounded by designer-clad white children who drink imported French water at their football games. I'm sure you know what's best for your own child.)

Whether you choose a state or a private school, it is now the norm for Mum and Dad to be busily running around the grounds, mentoring the dyslexic, watering the shrubbery, past-ing up the school newsletter, and generally making themselves very, very useful. If you are anything like me, the question you must be asking yourself is, 'How can I do, well, less?' Some of us opted out of getting a teaching credential, for the simple reason that we really don't want to spend that much time around young children. Some of us have Other Things to Do.

Having a full-time job might help you get out of some active volunteering, though you will probably be expected to give more money, and to share your expertise on Career Day. But perhaps you are in a freelance position, you are a 'writer' or some sort of 'creative artist'-type person. Just because you

may not work out of an 'office' in a fancy building doesn't mean you have hours and hours to devote to making birdhouses out of gourds with the reception class. You still need to have your uninterrupted cup of coffee in the morning while you mull over creative-type things. You still have your dreams, dreams for which you might one day get handsomely paid, at which time you will generously hand over truckloads of money for the new school library. In the meantime, you are finding it impossible to commit to steady volunteer work, though you know yourself to be a good person.

Much to my surprise, it turns out there are legions of eager mothers and fathers who volunteer at school as a way of life. You and I would only be in the way, doing something badly that others can do better and with far more enthusiasm. They actually don't want volunteers, and in fact they would prefer to take the extra job on themselves, at the same time letting people know how much of their time and energy they are devoting to the school.

Those pointed looks from the principal and the few minutes you must spend at the school auction to which you have donated nothing are a small price to pay for all those free mornings and early afternoons. Primary school will be over in no time, and then, thankfully, no one will want you around anymore. After all, you've already gone to school. Now it's somebody else's turn.

ON HELPING YOUR YOUNGSTER
WITH SCHOOL PROJECTS

START SAVING YOUR EMPTY SHOE BOXES NOW. EMPTY SHOE boxes fill a wide variety of project needs, from a clever Story-Time Diorama to a Valentine's Day postbox. The best way to secure enough shoeboxes is to continue to buy dozens of pairs of shoes. I know this may be difficult for some of you, but we all have to make sacrifices to ensure that our children are project-ready.

You may have occasionally to splurge on some really well made Italian footwear, which for some reason provides the sturdiest boxes, but it will all be worth it when you see the bright, shining look of accomplishment on the face of your child who has created an authentic 1:87 scale Viking ship for his World Explorers project out of a stalwart Prada shoe box. It's those little intangibles that make parenthood so worthwhile.

CHAPTER 19

SELF-ESTEEM AND OTHER
OVERRATED CONCEPTS

AS MUCH AS WE MUST ENCOURAGE OUR CHILDREN'S INTER-
ests and efforts, as much as we should praise them when they
work hard and do well, we do not need continually to assure
our wee ones that they are brilliant and can do no wrong, especially when they engage in an activity at which they are
mediocre, at best. It is not our job to protect our children from
every little slight and hurt and bad feeling.

The trouble starts with their first foray into competitive
sport: why do so many children break down in a fit of uncon-
trollable tears when they lose? Getting bowled out might hurt
their feelings, so Mummy and Daddy have shielded them from
the fact that there are outs at all. Being bowled out would
mean they did something wrong, and if they find out they don't
do everything perfectly, their whole world might crumble
around them.

Well, Mummy and Daddy, in cricket, as in life, there are
outs aplenty, and if your children learn this at a young age,
they will also learn how to simply enjoy the game.

Then there are the tiny trophies. Are these fine young athletes given tiny trophies because they have proven themselves to show particular prowess on the field or have demonstrated fine sportsmanship? No, they are given trophies simply for showing up. That, and the fact that Mum and Dad forked over a hundred pounds so that they could play in the first place. Some of these youngsters end up in the outfield, more intent upon looking for insects on the dandelions; others are in a cold sweat because their red-faced daddy is yelling at them to RUN!! RUN!! and they have no idea why they are supposed to run. They are tiny pawns in a game set up by the parents, for the parents, and gosh don't they look so cute in the kit! The children love their little trophies and, thinking that they've won something, continue with a sport most of them know or care little about.

Parents are basically bribing their children to play a game, a game that in other, simpler times, kids would race out of doors to play all by themselves. The game often involved a stick instead of a bat, and did not require the wearing of expensive replica kits. Kids played ball. It was *fun*. Then, when they had enough ball, they'd go and shoot some marbles, or look through their big brother's girlie magazines, or make up some game involving crumpled paper and an overturned lampshade.

What is winning without a million failures? Why have we made it so easy for children to succeed at everything, constantly lowering the bar so that their mere presence merits a gold statuette? If a child never accepts, or even embraces, his failures, what a blow it will be when one day he is teased, or rejected, or experiences one of the many failures that are simply part of the childhood itinerary.

Children need to earn their self-esteem, not be handed it on a platter. They are not stupid – most of them, anyway – and they secretly know that they really haven't done much to deserve all the accolades. And when they know they have done nothing spectacular, despite your praising them to the heavens, then you are, in fact, harming the very self-esteem you are trying so valiantly to build.

It is understandably disheartening to watch that lonely bowling ball rolling slowly down the gutter, but you are doing your child no favours by shielding him from the anguish of defeat. A few less trophies means fewer things on the shelf collecting dust, and just that much less housework for you.

The next time the children have a game of football in the garden and play with great enthusiasm (whether or not they play particularly well), bandy about phrases like 'Good job!' and 'Well done!' Unlike the ubiquitous trophies, these useful phrases take up no extra shelf space.

CHAPTER 20

KARATE, TENNIS, AND BALLET: YOUR CHILD'S EIGHTY-HOUR WORK WEEK

AH, SPRING. THE PINK BUDS BURSTING FORTH, THE SMELL of fresh-cut grass in the park, and the unmistakable refrain that tells us the tennis season is in full swing on the courts of Britain: the plaintive wail of a mother, calling to her child in the middle of the last exciting set, *'Ellie! Ellie! Come on, hurry up! Netball!'* And off little Ellie rushes, throwing the racquet to her mum and pulling the netball jersey over her tennis shirt. Learning a rich lesson in team loyalty as the minivan tears out of the car park.

Worried that your little one will somehow fall behind the curve if he is not being continually enriched, you sign your child up for football, yoga, basketball, and gymnastics. After all, his best friend plays a full complement of team sport, rounding out his Saturdays with violin lessons and art classes.

So each weekend finds you doing nothing but driving and bringing snacks to the various teams your child has been signed up for. On school nights, he often gets home from karate too late to do anything but wolf down some dinner and try to finish his homework. With two children, both parents are kept in a constant orbit, never stopping and rarely intersecting.

If you notice that it has been years since you saw your son or daughter sitting still for anything other than meals or homework, it is time to stop for a moment and assess the situation.

Do you find that you get nervous when you see your child simply doing nothing, that your left eye starts twitching when you see him lying on his back staring up at the ceiling? Take a long, deep breath. Walk away. Maybe he is thinking. Perhaps he is composing a song, or a poem. He might be following the path of a tiny spider as it makes its way across the moulding. He might be contemplating earwax and its many possible uses. It doesn't matter. Leave your child alone. Go and find something to do.

Your child is developing a necessary self-sufficiency, one that you will one day come to find very useful. One that you, perhaps, need to cultivate yourself.

It is not necessary that he be doing something educational and instructive every minute; nor are you required to clutter up your days, especially your weekends, driving from field to field, from activity to activity, so that you can watch your child have a Childhood Experience. If your child has a deep hunger to study the oboe or learn tap dancing, just be aware that when your child takes on a sport or an instrument, you are taking it on, too. Lessons and organized sport are enormous drains on your precious time, so you should think carefully before signing up. It is actually possible for your youngster to have a happy childhood without filling every spare moment with mandatory supervised activities.

It's often rather charming having the children around the house after school, and there is enormous satisfaction in keeping one's Saturdays and Sundays entirely free to potter in the garden, have a game of catch with your child, go to a farmers' market, or simply lounge about.

If you find that the children are lounging about too much, use their extra time at home to teach them all those little domestic skills that they will need so desperately later in life, skills that could even be of help to you. Do they know how to chill a glass properly or make decent canapés? Do they know any interesting uses for capers? If they've finished all their homework, run them through the domestic basics. Then send them into the other room with a good book. Reading is not only a highly enriching activity for your children, it also gets them out of your hair for a few hours, and requires no driving.

A Helpful Hint!

DO-IT-YOURSELF AFTER-SCHOOL EXTRACURRICULAR ACTIVITIES

1. *Care and Cleaning of Barware*
2. *Fun Foot Rubs for Mum and Dad!*
3. *Finding Good Hiding Places to Build Forts and Hide from Parents for Hours on End*
4. *Skedaddling for Beginners*
5. *Emptying the Dishwasher*
6. *The Meditative Qualities of Furniture Polishing*
7. *Hospital Corners and the Well-Made Bed*
8. *Make Yourself Scarce!*
9. *Weeding for Fun*
10. *Delicious Snacks for Mum and Dad*
11. *The Magic of Sock Sorting and Clothes Folding*
12. *The Art of Walking on Tiptoes*
13. *Chemistry in Action! The Gin Fizz*
14. *Letting Mummy Nap 101*

CHAPTER 21

STEPPIN' OUT WITH MY BABY

EATING OUT AT RESTAURANTS SHOULD NOT BE EXCLUSIVELY the province of those lucky few who have either regular baby-sitters or local relatives who enjoy watching their children. Dining out is a pleasure that should occasionally be shared with your child.

Helping children become accustomed to dining out as if they are actually civilized humans takes a bit of effort, but it will take much less effort if you begin when they are very young. While your child is still in a high chair, you needn't patronize five-star restaurants, but it is the time to eat out as often as possible, as you won't necessarily have to spring for any fourteen-pound entrées for your toddler. He will sit happily eating Cheerios out of a small bag, bang his cup a few times, and see contented parents enjoying food that they did not have to prepare, off plates that they will not have to wash. What a wonderful memory that will be for your child!

Take your children out to restaurants as often as you can afford it, but plan to eat early in the evening, especially on your first practice runs. Many of the diners taking advantage of early-bird dining specials may be hard of hearing, and may not notice your child if he should prove to be noisy or unmanageable. Five o'clock is the ideal time to perfect your child's restaurant etiquette. You will also find other families dining out at this time, so if your child behaves in a less than ideal manner, you won't be as conspicuous.

It would be best to assume that the charming couple across the room might not be delighted to have your child wander over to their table to pick food off their plates. By the same token, most restaurant goers will not find it adorable when that same child stands on his chair and announces, 'This food is revolting!' especially if they themselves have paid good money for a baby-sitter to watch their children for the evening. If your little one gets a quick game of peekaboo out of the sweet little girl in the next booth, he should count himself fortunate, and not press his luck.

Problems usually occur because toddlers, dining out their first few times, are unfamiliar with the lead time involved in ordering a meal. They want their spaghetti bolognese, and they expect it to appear as if by magic upon their arrival. Many family-friendly dining establishments offer their littlest patrons crayons, along with place mats that contain puzzles, join-the-dots pictures, and word games to take their minds off the fact that they have been sitting there for half an hour, and to keep them busy while you enjoy your nice glass of wine.

If one has chosen a restaurant that does not offer such diversions, there are a number of things one may do to keep a young child busy. If the restaurant uses paper place mats, then by all means bring along a nice ink pen or sharp pencil to give your child, and let him at it. Building sugar-packet skyscrapers is another good time filler, as is making words and letters out of toothpicks or, if you are getting Chinese, those little crispy noodles. If no tools are available, spelling out words in a layer of salt that you have shaken onto the tabletop is a sure crowd pleaser. Be sure to whisk it away before you vacate the table, or perhaps you could spell out a nice 'Thank you' for your waiter! If you are dining out in the most desirable residential area of a major city, then 'Spot the Face-lift' is a perennially entertaining pastime. Grown-ups can move on to the more challenging 'Spot the Botox', 'Spot the Collagen', and 'Are They Implants?' while quietly reminding the children not to point. Keep the pre-dinner games low in volume and short on strenuous activity, and save blowing the straw wrappers at one other for lunch at a casual, preferably outdoor spot.

Now, what if, after all this, your wilful two-year-old has decided that he has had enough? He screams, he stands on the chair, he barks out orders to his mother and father, he whines, most unpleasantly. He does not listen to you, or pay any attention to your repeated shushing and kicks under the table. If you are at a restaurant with your child by yourself, you might simply have to have your food wrapped up to take away and head home for a good nap. The sensible thing to do, if you are able, is to simply take your youngster out of doors for a nice little talk. He will find the sudden chill in the air rather bracing, and may be more amenable to discussing his unsociable behavior. He will also be deprived of his audience, in addition to being acutely aware that he is pacing up and down a dark street with a parent, and no doubt missing out on a load of good indoor fun. The change of scenery may snap him out of his mood, especially if coupled with threats of 'No story tonight', 'No cartoons on Saturday', or 'The bunny dies'.

Appeal to his developing sense of right and wrong, and encourage his emerging understanding of correct social behaviour, by reminding him that no one will want to take him out to nice restaurants if he makes life unpleasant for all the other nice people who are trying to have an agreeable and quiet dinner. Let him know that every time he behaves badly he will be silently and skilfully whisked out of the restaurant, into the cold, cold night, where he will be forced to listen to his dad or mum drone on and on about manners and being thoughtful towards our fellow diners. He should get the point rather quickly.

There are substantial rewards for training your child to be restaurant friendly. On those nights when you just can't manage either to cook or order another round of take-away, many more restaurant options will be available. You will not be limited to dining exclusively at establishments that cater to very young and fractious children, nor will you be forced into places where culinary excitement means pasty noodles smothered in orange goo, a fine film of which will usually be smeared on every surface. Your child might even learn to be an adventurous eater.

Enjoy your meal, and always leave a generous tip.

CHAPTER 22

TELEVISION:
IS SIX HOURS A DAY TOO MUCH?

SOME WELL-INTENTIONED BUT MISGUIDED PEOPLE BELIEVE that by denying a child access to commercial television, one is wilfully depriving him of a solid pop-culture education. Lacking basic television-watching skills, the poor child will be a social pariah at school, unable to join in on discussions regarding plot lines of the various popular programmes. 'Won't he feel alienated', they admonish, 'when he doesn't know what a Yugi-oh monster is, or how to catch a Pokémon?' as if this four-year-old will be standing alone by the watercooler while the happy and popular children discuss the finer points of Japanese animation.

First of all, unless your child is committed to the Amish life, he will simply know, through osmosis, detailed information about many popular children's television characters, without ever having seen a single programme. Go to any playground and you will find just as many children pretending to be Power Rangers as dinosaurs, and they need never have seen either one. They just know. It is difficult to eliminate completely the influence of television, but it can be lessened, simply by not allowing the TV to be a regular entertainment option.

I'm told that there is some really great viewing for children on television these days, shows that are intelligently written and contain fine messages for bright young minds. I choose to keep this information a secret from my own children. Television, preferably commercial-free television, certainly can be helpful to a new parent, and will enable you to have a quick shower and a slice of toast in the morning. A good video will also perform the same trick. But while it can be very effective in keeping a child happily occupied, you will end up a slave to the TV set and a slave to your child if she never learns to entertain herself. Trust me, the minute the TV programme or video is over, the call for 'Mummy!' will be heard, along with a demand for either Mummy's instant attention or another video. Give your children your full attention as often as you are able, but turn off the TV and help them discover the fun of playing by themselves, for their development as well as your own sanity.

That television watching remains a sedentary and passive pursuit is part of the problem, but even greater damage comes from the incessant and insidious commercials that will certainly turn your child into a rabid consumer, which ends up being very expensive for you, the parent. Keeping your children from watching the commercial television stations will at the very least ensure a holiday season relatively free of gift lists that have been culled straight from advertising campaigns and product tie-ins. Your children, unaware that they want and need entire collections of mutant action figures, adorable big-eyed dolls that are dressed to resemble teenage prostitutes, or fifteen incredibly violent video games, will be thrilled at the sight of a small bag of books, a handful of tiny cars, and a cuddly sock monkey – fine, thoughtful gifts that will cost you less than a cheap pedicure.

Understandably, if your child has been allowed to watch two or three hours of television every day for the past several years, it might be rather difficult when he is suddenly told that he may not do that anymore. Let me assure you that it is worth the effort. Here are a few TV-stopping arguments to attempt, if possible, while your child is still young and not yet addicted.

'It's a beautiful sunny day out, and we don't watch television on beautiful sunny days' is a useful phrase. This phrase, coupled with a look that says, 'Of course *you* are clever enough to know *that*', should be gently repeated every time a whining request to watch TV is heard. If you are not fortunate enough to live in a temperate climate or if it is, in fact, raining out, you may amend the admonition to 'We don't watch television during the *day*, of course you know that'. The word 'television' must be said with an understated, polite disdain, as if you are sniffing what might be the faint odour of a dead rodent under the subflooring. For practice, substitute the phrase 'we don't eat candy floss for breakfast', and you will understand the inflection of incredulity that is required. Unless you do eat candy floss for breakfast, in which case there's no reasoning with you.

A videotape on a weekend night, as a special treat, is fine. Or if, during the week, you have company and want to socialize without the aid of small children. Children whose daily exposure to television has been severely curtailed not only avoid a lifetime of obesity, diabetes and bloodshot eyes, they usually develop quite impressive attention spans. When they are allowed a film only as a special treat, they will generally watch the entire film in a single sitting, a real bonus when your dinner party is running late.

CHAPTER 23

YOUR COST-EFFECTIVE TOMBOY

I CRINGE WHEN I SEE AN OTHERWISE HEALTHY GIRL OF seven or eight struggling through the sand at the playground in a pair of pink glitter platform sandals. I won't even mention the skintight capris and midriff-baring tube top, as there is no need for me to foist my taste on some poor child who obviously lacks a basic fashion sense. The pink and the glitter raise another problem entirely, but when it comes to shoes, Mothers and Fathers, might we attempt to have a modicum of reason? If your daughter is five, or six, or even ten, she should be wearing comfortable, flat, sensible shoes, shoes that allow a young girl to engage in child-friendly activities, shoes that do not make her dependent upon you to simply help her move from one spot to another. Shoes that will not put her in an unattractive neck brace in her formative years.

I have seen little girls as young as four teetering on wildly inappropriate footwear, and the sight brings to mind nothing so much as the tiny bound feet of a Chinese concubine. Your daughter might think a pair of three-inch platform mules the height of smartness, and I'm sure she believes she *must* have them, but by actually allowing her to mince around in such impractical footwear, you are denying her some of the simple pleasures of childhood: racing on the beach, climbing trees, jumping off the monkey bars, skipping across the pavement, running upstairs to retrieve your book and into the kitchen to fetch you a nice cold drink. She will be limited to walking gingerly, standing around in shopping centres, and trying not to tip over in high winds. Imagine who will eventually have to pay for the inevitable orthopaedic and chiropractic help that she will require.

Stupid shoes should be the prerogative of women over the age of nineteen, after they have given it much thought and undergone a certain amount of training in the privacy of their own homes.

If your child is already a pint-sized fashion addict, it may be too late, but if she is still fairly young, here are a few techniques you might try to help create your own cost-effective tomboy.

Sport. Encourage an interest in sport. Watch athletics competitions and admire the strapping gals in utilitarian shoes. Marvel at their jumping skills, and point out that girls who wear platforms on their feet generally aren't much for jumping. Care must be taken, however, to keep her from watching the advertisements that are ubiquitous to sports programming, as she may be confused by the sudden images of underfed, large-breasted blondes in high heels and bikinis, selling beer and cars. Safer to rent *Babe!*, a fine biopic about Babe Didrikson.

Folk Music. Encourage the singing and playing of folk songs. Folk singers who espouse environmentalism, women's rights, and civil liberty are rarely found teetering on four-inch Manolo Blahniks. Look for modern folk artists who wear their lefty politics on their sweatshirt sleeves, along with a sensible pair of blue jeans and trainers.

Films. Watch films with populist themes and strong female characters. Think Jean Arthur rather than Jean Harlow. As far as the various Hepburns, both Katharine and Audrey, who were big on flat shoes and trousers, and are perfect role models for being stylish *and* practical.

Negotiating the landscape in high heels is a highly skilled but dangerous art form, and it is best left to professional dancers and vocational streetwalkers. However, playing 'dressing up' is a fine activity, and I encourage you occasionally to lend your daughter that pair of stilettos you bought ages ago but can't seem to throw away. She will be able to traipse around the house in a safe environment and have the thrill of wearing ridiculous shoes, while you will have a justification for keeping those shoes in the cupboard a little bit longer, just in case you need them.

CHAPTER 24

DON'T, LIKE, WASTE MY TIME

IT IS A SAD FACT OF LIFE THESE DAYS THAT SPEECH PAT-
terns once relegated to the rarefied province of thirteen-year-
old girls from a certain enclave of Southern California are now
heard in schools across the country. I, like, find it, like, rather
disturbin'? That, like, girls as young as five years old? Don't
understand that when they, like, grow up? That no matter how
educated they become, if they don't, like, break this irritating
habit, then, like, they run the risk of sounding forever like a,
like, nitwit?

For you, the parent, your child sounding like a nitwit is,
in fact, the least annoying part of this problem. It is the precious time it takes out of your day to have to listen to a child
get through what could be said in a few well-chosen words.

When your child shows a propensity for incorrectly and
incessantly using the word 'like', she must be stopped. If she
uses the word 'like' in any way other than comparing two
things, in the judicious use of simile, or as a term of endearment,
she must be set straight. Correct her at every turn. Correct her
to the point of acute embarrassment, if need be.

'So, I'm like, that is, like, *such* a cool car? and he's like –'

'Was it *like* a cool car, or *was* it a cool car?'

'Mum, okay. It was a cool car. So then, I'm like, Jessica –'

'*Like* Jessica, or Jessica?'

'Jessica! OKAY!! Anyway, so I go to Jessica, I go, You *so* have to come over after school, and she goes –'

'Excuse me, you *go* where? She goes where? Where did you both *go*?'

'She *says*. Come on, Mum, just forget it. FORGET IT.'

Which is fine, because it truly was an inane story that you really didn't want to hear. The time you will have saved over a period of ten years in not having to listen to the word 'like' in between every other word could probably add up to a nice weekend in Prague.

Another alternative, although it really should be a last resort, is to mimic the speaker until she hears how silly she sounds. This may only work with certain pre-teens and teenagers, and they must be familiar with your sarcastic nature before it can be effective. (I tried it once on a forty-year-old acquaintance, mocking her mercilessly, and she simply thought I was enthusiastically agreeing with her.)

Be careful, however. If you engage in the above exercise you may not be able to stop. Just as a nursery teacher may find it difficult to stop humming the alphabet song, you may find yourself unable to shed this frighteningly addictive habit. This is why so many people, like, speak this way. Grown friends of mine do it; my sisters do it. It makes me insane, but nonetheless I find myself slipping into the hated vernacular, just as one will speak the slang of any given region if one is visiting for a long period. Do not visit this region for long. It is deadly. It is as bad as starting an Irish brogue in a room full of actors. As an antidote, fall asleep at night to the soothing tones of the BBC news. You will catch up on the day's events while simultaneously tuning your ear to the sounds of well-spoken English.

CHAPTER 25

THE AMAZING HANDS-OFF DADDY

IT MIGHT SEEM SURPRISING TO SOME, BUT THERE ARE A great many daddies who are not, as we have been led to believe, right in there with the girls, changing nappies, disciplining their tots, and generally co-shouldering the burdens of laundry, baby bathing, cooking, and keeping the house somewhat clutter free. This particular breed of male was there to experience the miracle of birth at the side of his partner, an experience that he secretly found messy and alarming, but since then he's been hoping that there will be ways to stay on the sidelines and avoid the onslaught of unfamiliar and unwanted duties.

Ladies, no one ever asks us if we would like to take a few years off from household and child rearing duties. If both Mummy and Daddy are parties in having the child, then both really should have to do the job together. I'm sure Mr Man works long and hard at a job outside the house, but he must know that whatever important work he has is a walk in the park compared to caring for a toddler all day long. This type of father needs a short round of training, and if he is naturally resistant to lifting a finger, the training must be started early.

You could try holding up a nappy with a sweet, helpless look that says, 'Um, darling? I have completely forgotten how this thing works', and see if he will jump to your aid; but he is probably a master of that particular game and may not fall for it. What you need to do is to take a day off. Every week. Let him sleep in on Saturday, and you get to sleep in on Sunday. When you do get up, make yourself scarce – the day is yours. Leave a list of suggestions for him, should he run into trouble, including but not limited to:

1. Feed child breakfast.
2. Tell child no when child demands biscuits for breakfast.
3. Deal with child's tantrum.
4. Help child brush teeth.
5. Help child wipe after pooing.
6. Take child to park.
7. Talk to child about importance of sharing.
8. Put bandage on scraped knee. (They're in the medicine cabinet!)
9. Make child lunch. Include some sort of 'fresh' foods.
10. Wash dirty park clothes along with a load of laundry.
11. Play game of some sort.

12. Put out child's crayons and paper. (While child is drawing, use the bathroom, brush your own teeth, etc.)
13. Wash child's sticky hands.
14. Make a snack.
15. Read child favourite books.
16. Take child to library for more books.
17. Make child dinner. Include some 'vegetables'.
18. Encourage child to eat dinner.
19. Help child to brush teeth.
20. Read child new favourite books.
21. Tuck child in.
22. Cuddle, and administer good-night kisses.

On your day off, do not put yourself in rescuing distance. Forget to bring your mobile phone. Do an activity that enables you to use both arms freely. Eat a meal slowly. Have a leisurely conversation with another adult. You don't always have to disappear for an entire day, and in fact you might want to do some things as a family on weekend afternoons, but in order for your spouse to gain a complete understanding and appreciation of the job, he must really experience a full day of child care. Assume that he is eager to spend an entire day with his child, as he has seen so little of the tyke all week. In addition to taking a weekly day off, give your partner a shopping list once in a while. Suggest that he try his hand at cooking a dinner, one that doesn't involve barbecue or spaghetti.

I know a handful – a very small handful – of men who actually do carry half the load or more, and I mean making the shopping list, not just going to the shop. Knowing where the children keep their art supplies and favourite toys, handling a load of laundry with aplomb, and generally doing what needs to be done.

These are the quiet heroes who will read books to the kids without talking about whose 'turn' it is. The fine men who do not have to call their wives frantically after fifteen minutes of being alone with their progeny because their child has peed on the floor. Those admirable men who don't expect a hearty round of applause for their amazing display of sensitivity and strength after they manage to do the tiniest thing related to the keeping of the house and children. The ones who have really bonded with their children, because they have been there for the good and the bad.

For all the daddies out there who either take care of their child full-time or contribute more than their share of the domestic duties, I salute you, and I can't tell you what a joy it is to be married to one of you. Carry on, and continue to show your sons and daughters what a real man is made of.

WHY DO WE HAVE CHILDREN?

BECAUSE IT JUST SEEMED LIKE 'A GOOD IDEA' OR BECAUSE one day, having run out of conversation, one of us said, 'It's time'. Sometimes it's because the moon was bright, and the lights were low, and the cable went out for the night. Perhaps there was an earthquake, or a blackout, or you both polished off a nice bottle of Château Margaux '79, and here you are, nine months later, with slightly astonished looks on your faces. The point is, people have been bearing and raising live young since the beginning of time, which is why we are all here, after all. Yes, each tiny baby is a miracle, and yes, they are, in fact, wee and precious, but so were you at that age, and now look at yourself.

Certainly being a parent is a responsibility not to be taken lightly, but honestly, when all is said and done, children are nice to have around for the cuddling, and so that one can experience the joy of reading *Guess How Much I Love You* hundreds and hundreds of times, and because we can get them to do extra chores for us once in a while. We should attempt to share whatever wisdom we might have accidentally accumulated, and we should try to help them become nice people, because very quickly they will be big, and then they'll be gone. We should not waste those scant eighteen or so years worrying about things over which we have little or no control.

One day you will wake up and go to make breakfast for your child, and he will have already wolfed down a smoothie and nine scrambled eggs because he will be seventeen. You will offer to drive him to his football practice, and he will explain that he's getting a lift with his pal Jack. You tell him that you're going to drop by his school to watch him present his political science report, and he will roll his eyes and tell you to read it instead, and you will ask him to bring all of his friends over after practice for 'a pizza party!' and he will tell you, in as nice a way as possible, to 'get a life, Mum'. With this book I am really just trying to give you a head start, to make sure you have some sort of life on which to fall back when that day arrives.

And when that day arrives, you will need friends, and a proper social life, and perhaps a hobby, and you will not have these things if you have spent the last seventeen years alienating your friends and neglecting your social life. Do not make your child your only hobby or you will end up waiting by the telephone in a cheery room covered in brittle, yellowed crayon drawings, regaling those few friends that are left with stale anecdotes about your youngster's accomplishments. Your little baby will be off at university, or backpacking in the Amazon, or on the other side of the country trying to get as far away from home as possible, and you will begin collecting porcelain frogs and feeding stray cats. So now is the time to start getting that life to fall back on. You know what you must do. Do it for your child. Do it for me, and for everyone out there who has to deal with your child for the rest of your child's life. And do it for yourself.

Cheers!